101 mathematical projects:
a resource book

Brian Bolt
David Hobbs

KU-670-320

CAMBRIDGE
UNIVERSITY PRESS

CAMBRIDGE UNIVERSITY PRESS
Cambridge, New York, Melbourne, Madrid, Cape Town, Singapore, São Paulo

Cambridge University Press
The Edinburgh Building, Cambridge CB2 2RU, UK

www.cambridge.org
Information on this title: www.cambridge.org/9780521347594

© Cambridge University Press 1989

This book is in copyright. Subject to statutory exception
and to the provisions of relevant collective licensing agreements,
no reproduction of any part may take place without
the written permission of Cambridge University Press.

First published 1989
12th printing 2005

Printed in the United Kingdom at the University Press, Cambridge

A catalogue record for this publication is available from the British Library

ISBN-13 978-0-521-34759-4 paperback
ISBN-10 0-521-34759-9 paperback

Illustrations by Ian Dicks, Tony Hall, Nigel Luckhurst,
Amanda MacPhail, Nick May and Neil Sutton

Contents

Introduction

In the UK a series of reports on the teaching of mathematics has highlighted the short-comings of learning mathematical techniques in isolation. The result of this has been a set of national criteria for the teaching of mathematics which emphasises the need for pupils to be taught in such a way that they will be able to use the mathematics they learn. This has been followed by new school-leaving examinations involving coursework projects to promote this aim. To most teachers this means a significant change in what is demanded of them. We whole-heartedly support the change in emphasis in mathematics education but we are also aware of the problems which its implementation will inevitably bring. With this in mind we have drawn on our many years in teacher training to produce this resource book of over a hundred topics which we believe teachers will find invaluable when they introduce coursework.

Brian Bolt
David Hobbs
University of Exeter
School of Education

Why coursework?

In recent years there has been a growing recognition that pupils should learn mathematics in such a way that they can see its relevance to the world in which they live and be able to use it to gain a better appreciation of that world. Often mathematics has been learned as a set of routines to be carried out blindly in response to stereotyped exam questions. The result of such teaching and learning is that pupils are unable to apply their knowledge outside the standard textbook sums. Further, the motivation for learning becomes largely dependent on getting the ticks corresponding to right answers and has little to do with any intrinsic interest in the subject or whether or not the answer is meaningful.

When mathematics is taught in that way pupils rarely, if ever, have opportunity to ask their own questions. The questions come to them from textbook exercises, workcards or worksheets, or exam papers, and no matter how carefully they have been designed they have come from an external source beyond pupils' control.

The way in which pupils are ultimately assessed has a very strong influence on the way in which mathematics is taught. As long as the school-leaving assessment is based on timed written papers with a large number of questions to be answered then little will change. Fortunately for the future of mathematics in the UK this has now been recognised.

The Cockcroft Report: *Mathematics Counts* (HMSO 1982) spelt out, among other things, that mathematics teaching at all levels should include: discussion, practical work, investigational work, problem solving, and application of mathematics to everyday situations.

The HM Inspectorate developed the ideas inherent in the Cockcroft Report in their discussion document: *Mathematics from 5 to 16* (HMSO 1985) where they spelt out a set of aims and objectives including the need to develop independent thinking:

There is a danger that mathematics might be made to appear to pupils to consist mainly of answering set questions, often of a trivial nature, to which the answers are already known and printed in the answer book! But *pupils will have developed well mathematically when they are asking and answering their own questions . . . why? . . . how? . . . what does that mean? . . . is there a better way? . . . what would happen if I changed that? . . . does the order matter? . . .*

Parallel to these reports has come the development of National Criteria for secondary mathematics, and a new examination, the General Certificate for Secondary Education (GCSE) to be taken at 16+.

In the introduction to the National Criteria for mathematics it states that any scheme of assessment must:

(a) assess not only the performance of skills and techniques but also pupils' understanding of mathematical processes, their ability to make use of these processes in the solution of problems and their ability to reason mathematically;

(b) encourage and support the provision of courses which will enable pupils to develop their knowledge and understanding of mathematics to the full extent of their capabilities, to have experience of mathematics as a means of solving practical problems and to develop confidence in their use of mathematics.

It has been appreciated that these aims cannot all be met by written papers but are best met by an element of coursework done in the two years prior to the examination. This coursework element cannot be obtained by accumulating pieces of homework or tests but is to consist of practical work and investigations which require independence and initiative on the part of the individual. The term 'extended piece of work' is used and this has the valuable ingredient of a task performed over a significant period of time, a feature lacking when work is set on one day and collected in on the next.

Suggested activities include

(a) problems or tasks, which because they are unfamiliar, give opportunity to develop initiative and flexibility and so encourage a spirit of enquiry;
(b) tasks in which a variety of strategies and skills can be used;
(c) problems and surveys in which information has to be gathered and inferences have to be made;
(d) situations which can be investigated, with opportunities for strategies such as trial and error and searching for pattern;
(e) extended pieces of work which enable a pupil to investigate a topic or problem at length;
(f) opportunities for pupils to generate their own investigative activities.

However, as is pointed out, the ability to carry out these activities loses much unless the pupils can communicate their findings to others. It follows that pupils need to develop the ability to describe what they have achieved using words, diagrams, graphs or formulae as appropriate. And last but not least they are to be encouraged to talk about their findings.

This coursework element seems a daunting task to teachers whose main concern has been to prepare pupils for written examinations. Many find themselves having to teach in ways which they have not themselves experienced when pupils, so they have no model to fall back on. Inservice courses are helpful as pump priming exercises but in the end a teacher needs a source of ideas presented in a form which can be readily used with pupils. It was with this in mind that this book has been written. It contains many topics, giving ways in which they may be developed, and the kinds of questions which pupils can be encouraged to ask and seek answers to. Many of the topics can be developed in a variety of ways and the depth and width of any project based on them will depend on the ability of the pupil concerned and the time scale envisaged for the project to be completed. The range of topics included has been chosen to cater for a variety of interests and to cover a wide range of concepts and skills.

Teachers often look for a situation to illustrate or motivate an interest in a piece of mathematics which they want to introduce. This is still relevant, but in doing the coursework element of GCSE it should be the intrinsic interest and relevance of the problem which takes precedence, not the mathematics.

In writing this book we have concentrated on projects which have links with the real world to emphasise the relevance of mathematics to a better understanding of our environment. We have consciously omitted the pure mathematics investigations such as those involving number patterns or shape, unless they have tangible links with real problems, as these are already well resourced. We have thus grouped the project topics into themes such as measurement, sport, the home, transport and technology rather than into topics such as statistics, scale drawing, and algebra. The situation should determine what aspects of mathematics are used and in most cases several techniques will be involved. For example a project based on sport may look at the characteristics of a bouncing ball and involve designing an experiment, measuring, graphical representation and a theoretical model *or* it may make a study of the effect of different scoring systems on the outcome of sporting competitions and suggest possible alternatives with an analysis of the likely outcome of their implementation.

The level of mathematics in a project will often be quite low. In practice much of the mathematical content of a project is likely to consist of activities such as: estimating, measuring, collecting and recording data, drawing graphs, scale drawings, and straightforward arithmetic. It is in the planning of the project, the design of an experiment, the search for information, the questions asked, the conclusions formed, and the communication of the findings where this aspect of the mathematics course differs from the traditional curriculum.

The research of the Assessment of Performance Unit (APU) which regularly monitors pupils' performance in mathematics also assesses their attitude to the subject. It shows that the single most significant factor in creating a positive attitude to mathematics is a pupil's perception of the usefulness of the subject. This is true whether or not a child finds the subject easy, and it becomes more marked as a child grows older. The traditional secondary school mathematics curriculum has always attempted to show mathematics to be useful, but the questions were often contrived to try to use the mathematics being taught or on topics like 'stocks and shares' which could hardly seem relevant to a sixteen-year-old. The questions and examples were imposed from outside. Now there is the opportunity, which teachers must rapidly acknowledge, of allowing pupils to tackle their own problems and in so doing grow in independence and confidence and make the subject their own.

The essence of this book is in the project outlines but some guidelines are given towards starting project work and how to assess the results. Further we give a list of useful resource books and materials. By the time teachers have been involved in coursework for a few years they will realise how limitless is the list of starting points for pupils' coursework. Meanwhile we believe we have put together a wide ranging set of starting points which will give confidence to teachers embarking on this work and add to the possibilities of those with some experience.

Introducing coursework in the classroom

The examining boards' coursework requirements normally refer to assignments carried out in the two years leading up to the final examination date. However, it would be a grave mistake to delay the start of project work to this stage. Many pupils will have been involved in project work in their primary schools, so it would be advantageous to see project work introduced in the first year of secondary school and to be an ever-present element of the mathematics course.

Because the introduction of project work has been initiated, in many cases, by the requirements of an examination, there is often an unhealthy concern with assessment and this tends to dominate teachers' discussions. This is unfortunate. Projects should first and foremost be about getting pupils involved as independent thinkers, asking questions, making and testing hypotheses, collecting data, forming conclusions, and communicating their findings. The emphasis on assessment leads to a concern with making sure that work is only that of an individual when it would be far better to encourage cooperative effort and team work. With this last point in mind we would suggest that, in many cases, project work should be planned and carried out by teams of pupils. This makes sense for example in measuring activities or traffic surveys, and in many practical situations. In fact the discussion between the members of a team and their joint planning is an invaluable part of this aspect of the course.

Take, for example, the problems of car parking. There are many aspects of this, and following a class discussion to identify specific problems, teams of three or four could be formed to pursue them in more detail. The teams would be expected to do what was necessary to analyse their problems and then present their findings to the rest of the class. This presentation could be in the form of a written or oral report, or a wall display or a model or using a micro. One team, for example, might make a study of a local car park, another look at street parking and another at the possibilities of forming a car park from the school playground for a special function. Such a topic will involve measurement, data collection, surveying, graphs, planning and decision making to name just a few of the skills, and if it can be linked to a real problem so much the better.

Some projects, such as a statistical analysis of the contents of different newspapers, can easily be carried out by individuals but would be more rewarding if done by groups of pupils because of the inevitable discussion which will arise and the saving in time on what could become a repetitive and possibly boring task for an individual. In a group there will always be someone who does more than their fair share and someone who takes a back seat, but that is life, and learning how to work as a team is as important a skill to acquire as the insights gained into using mathematics. Pupils too are often more ready to discuss and learn from each other than from the teacher.

The new Scottish Standard Grade has incorporated practical investigations and makes the point of the desirability of working together to develop social and personal qualities. It also includes the following relevant paragraph:

Working co-operatively with others is a powerful way of tackling problems. Moreover, the exchange of ideas through discussion is an essential part of learning. Activities are required to develop the ability to work with others towards a common goal, or for a common purpose.

One problem which arises from group work is how much each individual is expected to record. Is a group project a shared experience which only lives on in the memory of the individuals or does each person write up a complete report? Projects must be viewed positively by both pupils and teachers and must not become a burden. On the other hand, if detailed reports are not produced the activities will become rather pointless. A compromise must be found, and one solution is for a detailed write-up to be produced by a group which is available for all to see, together with skeleton reports with the main results and conclusions which each pupil can keep in their coursework file.

It is not easy to generalise about how to set about doing a project. In the beginning it will help if the projects are carefully structured and fairly limited in scope. They may well be closely linked to the mathematics syllabus being taught at the time, but pupils will be able to show more independence if the projects in which they are involved depend more on using mathematics in which they are already reasonably competent. Later the projects can be much more open-ended and may in fact be proposed by the pupils themselves. The choice of topic for a project will influence to some extent the stages involved but the following framework is offered as a guideline:

1 Interpreting the task

Having chosen a topic the first stage is to come to terms with what might be involved. What kinds of question can be asked? What information is given or is readily available? What can be measured? What data can be collected? Who might have relevant information? What has the library to offer?

2 Selecting a line of attack

Having taken in the possibilities of the situation some decision has to be made as to which particular aspect attention should be focussed on. Pupils may initially be tempted into trying to be too comprehensive in their approach and will need guidance to narrow down and define a problem which is sufficiently limited for them to achieve a result before they lose interest.

3 Planning and implementation

Having decided on a strategy the need is then to implement it. What information is required and how will it be obtained? How will measurements be made or data collected and how will it be recorded? Who is available to help and when will be a suitable time to carry out any survey? What equipment will be needed and from where can it be obtained?

At this stage it could be helpful to write down, possibly in the form of a flow diagram, what needs to be done and who will do it, before any action takes place.

4 Recording and processing

When the data is collected it needs to be recorded in a meaningful form. This might be, for example, in a table, a bar chart, a pie chart, or a scatter diagram. The processing may involve drawing graphs, calculating means, making models or computing. Questions may arise about relationships between sets of data, and hypotheses can be proposed and tested.

5 Extension

In the process of doing a project it is quite likely that further or related questions propose themselves which could be pursued or presented as problems requiring further research.

6 Presentation

When writing up a report it is helpful for the pupils to see themselves as consultants writing a document for a third party, rather like a surveyor might write a report on a house for a possible purchaser. The result of a project may end up as a scale drawing, say of a proposed house extension, or a series of models to demonstrate how shapes fill space or how folding push-chairs operate. Alternatively a wall display with pictograms and pie charts of a statistical survey or a display of patchwork patterns with an analysis of the unit of design may be more appropriate. But presentations could well include expositions by individuals or teams making use of the blackboard, OHP, models or any form of visual aid they can devise. Opportunities to communicate their findings in this way with the follow-up questions from their peer group would take time but could be an invaluable part of the exercise.

The teacher's role in project work is all important. To start with it is probably easier for the teacher to give the same project to all the pupils, so that setting the scene has only to be done once, and for the teacher to keep close control over its development. Take, for example, project 10 based on bouncing balls. After an initial discussion with the class about the wide range of balls used in different sports pupils should become aware of the need to find a way of measuring how well a ball bounces, and the need for manufacturers to produce balls with a consistent bounce for each sport. From this discussion should emerge the idea of dropping a ball from a known height and seeing to what height it bounces as a suitable way of measuring a ball's bounciness. The teacher will need to have available a number and range of balls together with measuring tapes or metre rules so that the class can divide up into groups of three to investigate the characteristics of balls such as:

- How does the bounce of a ball change with the height from which it is dropped?
- How does the bounce of a ball change with the surface onto which it is dropped?
- Which bounces best, a marble, a golf ball, or a netball?

A double period should be sufficient to get this project off the ground and it should end with a feedback session where each group briefly reports on their findings to date. This could be followed by homework where each pupil (a) writes about why manufacturers need to be able to measure the bounce of a ball and (b) describes the experiment they have carried out together with their results and conclusions.

The project could stop at this point, but much more is achieved if at least another double period is given over to it when groups could (a) try to answer for themselves the questions previously tackled by the other groups and (b) look at other related problems such as the lengths of consecutive bounces, the bounce of a ball off a racket or the effect of temperature.

Following this it would be helpful for the pupils if the teacher constructs a set of notes on the board, from class discussion, which sets out the main questions investigated and the conclusions found together with further questions yet to be answered.

At this stage the assessment takes a back seat, but from joint efforts of this kind pupils will develop an understanding of how to approach and write up a project, so that from being largely teacher led the move can be gradually made over the years to the projects being almost entirely dependent on individual pupils. A class may, for example, be given a choice of doing a project on the postal service, or the milk supply, or waste disposal, and initially be given a free hand as to what to do, only being offered advice or possible approaches as the need arises. This kind of project will necessarily take place largely in the pupils' own time for it will require the search for facts outside of school. In this case a time limit should be given, say three weeks, in which no other mathematics homework is set, and opportunities given in class throughout this time to talk with individuals about their progress and to give encouragement and suggest references. Pupils should be encouraged to discuss their projects with each other and share findings but, in the end, which aspects of the situation a pupil investigates and the way it is written up will be very much the work of an individual.

Only in the final years when the projects are to be assessed as part of an external examination is it necessary to ensure that the work written up and assessed is the unaided work of the pupil concerned. But 'unaided' is not easy to define, for if a pupil shows enough initiative to seek out people who are knowledgeable and can suggest ideas to improve their project this should be applauded. What we are really looking for is that a pupil has come to terms with the project and the write-up is their own.

As pupils become more experienced in pursuing projects the teacher can keep a low profile. Having initiated a project the pupils should try to ask the questions and provide the answers. Teachers should encourage, give advice, and make suggestions but they need to try above all to leave the initiative and responsibility for their projects with the pupils. Our experience is that when pupils are given this responsibility they often surprise themselves, let alone their teachers, with what they achieve. But don't expect too much too soon! In the early stages the projects should be structured by the teacher after discussion with the class and gradually the pupils can be given more independence.

The best way to get a pupil involved is often to start with a pupil's interest or hobby whether it is stamp collecting, cycling or pop music. In this way they will approach project work with confidence for they will have something to contribute and often be in the position of being more knowledgeable than you, the teacher. Then it will be your role to help them to develop a worthwhile project around their chosen area by asking questions as an interested outsider. The only danger in this approach is that you may end up with an interesting account of a person's hobby but with little or no mathematics. So be warned, and try to point your pupils towards some aspect of their hobbies which can be quantified.

Projects are an excellent vehicle for cooperative work, they also give opportunity for practising basic skills in a meaningful context, but in selecting projects it is well to remember the statement emphasised in the Cockcroft Report:

We believe it should be a fundamental principle that no topic should be included unless it can be developed sufficiently for it to be applied in ways in which the pupil can understand.

This statement refers to mathematical topics but it clearly expresses the philosophy which we believe should permeate the teaching of mathematics, and the projects will be the medium through which most pupils will be able to demonstrate their understanding of mathematics.

Assessment

Not only does the inclusion of coursework in mathematics syllabuses bring a different emphasis to the *learning* of mathematics, giving students opportunity to investigate and apply mathematics themselves, it also requires a different style of *assessment*.

In mathematics examinations the mark schemes have always been carefully laid down and marking has been as objective as possible. It is therefore not easy for mathematics teachers to adapt to a less precise style, although it should be remembered that marking in other fields such as Art, English and History has always involved a certain amount of subjectivity.

Clearly it is necessary at a national level to provide assessment criteria for coursework which can command respect. The dilemma is that over-prescription of the coursework content and of the assessment criteria will prevent the aims of the coursework from being realised. As the Northern Examining Association says in its GCSE syllabus (1988):

Coursework is envisaged as enhancing both the curriculum and the assessment. It is seen as a means of widening the scope of the examination and of providing an opportunity for the assessment of mathematical abilities which cannot easily be assessed by means of written papers. The aim is one of making what is important measurable rather than of making what is measurable important. The incorporation of a coursework element in the GCSE Mathematics examination is seen, therefore, as being concerned with pedagogy at least as much as it is with assessment.

The development of criteria

For teachers who do not have much experience of coursework we suggest that they begin with younger children where it is not necessary to give such a high priority to assessment, rather than at the fifteen- and sixteen-year-old stage. At first it might be advisable to begin with short activities before launching out on some of the more extended projects. For example, an activity accessible to eleven- and twelve-year-olds is to design a book of stamps (see project 60). This could begin with a discussion about points such as:
- the cost of the book (50p, £1, £2, £5?);
- useful values of stamps to be included (based on current first and second class postage rates);
- size of the book (number of stamps per page? number of pages?)

The possibilities for one particular cost could then be analysed by discussion with the whole class. Pupils could then try it out for another cost, working in small groups or for homework. A comparison with the books produced by the Post Office could be made and some market research could take place to find which of various possibilities was the most popular. The results could be written up as a report or as a wall display.

As experience is gained it could be that with eleven- to fourteen-year-olds one project is carried out each term, occupying the lessons for one or two weeks, with the children working, where appropriate, in groups. The outcome would be a presentation of some form: a display of models, wall charts, written booklets, etc. possibly accompanied by a verbal account. The teacher could then initiate a discussion about the projects bringing out points such as:
- Did the group members plan their work carefully?
- Were they correct in what they did?
- Did they present their findings in a clear way?

The achievements of each group would thus be made public, aiming for a mature attitude of help and cooperation. Through these discussions pupils could come to appreciate the standards to aim for and the main criteria on which assessment could be based. As the pupils gain experience they could assess the work of other groups on agreed criteria using, say, a five-point scale. By the fourth and fifth years students should then be capable of conducting projects on an individual basis and should appreciate how they will be assessed.

Some guidelines

The following guidelines are offered for assessment of projects:

1 In looking at a completed project the most obvious feature is the *presentation*:
   - Does it communicate?
   - Is it clearly expressed?
   - Are diagrams, tables, models, etc. clear?
   - Has it been carefully put together?

2 A more detailed study of the project involves consideration of its *content*:
   - Have relevant questions been posed?
   - Has appropriate information been obtained and used?
   - Have appropriate mathematical ideas been used?
   - Is the mathematics correct?
   - Have conclusions been drawn?
   - Have extensions been undertaken?

3 In some cases it might be appropriate to give credit for the *doing* of the project:
   - Was it initiated by the pupil?
   - Was teacher support needed?
   - Did the pupils develop their own strategy?
   - Is there evidence of personal initiative?

Major categories such as these could be assessed on a five-point numerical scale, say, and the results combined, with suitable weightings, to give an overall assessment. Different weightings might be appropriate depending on the ability level of the children. Care is needed in matching projects to pupils especially when they have freedom to choose their own projects. For less able children the projects need to be within their capabilities: project 30, 'Decorating and furnishing a room', offers possibilities for such children. For able children the projects must have potential for involving mathematics at a suitably high level and this should be looked for in the assessment scheme: see, for example, project 79, 'Packing', and project 89, 'Crystals' (second part) where the demands on spatial thinking are high. In some cases it might be that a project can be developed at various levels: project 23, 'Designing games of chance', can be taken at a simple level or extended to games which require careful analysis using probabilistic ideas.

In conclusion, we would like to emphasise again that assessment must be the servant of the curriculum and that what is taught should not be tailored to those aspects of the curriculum which can be measured easily. We would therefore wish to encourage teachers to experiment and, where examining boards allow, to produce their own style of coursework and appropriate assessment. Also, we hope that there would not be a dichotomy between projects and other forms of teaching. Rather, we would hope that an atmosphere of discussion, investigation and problem solving, as we have tried to indicate in the projects, would pervade the teaching of all of the mathematics.

The projects

The projects outlined on the following pages have been classified under a number of headings in order to give structure to the book. Some of these headings correspond to areas specified by the GCSE examination groups.

The projects have deliberately been chosen on a great variety of topics. Clearly not all the examples will appeal to everyone. It is certainly not intended that pupils should work through them systematically. We would like to encourage recognition of the fact that pupils are different and that the work they do in mathematics should match their abilities and interests. Some of the suggestions are at quite a low level while others involve difficult mathematical ideas and are only suitable for the most able students.

In some examples we have tried to encourage an across-the-curriculum approach. For example, there are links with subjects such as Art, Biology, Chemistry, CDT, Geography, Music and Physics. This allows children whose main interest is in some other school subject to build on it in their mathematics lessons. Advice from teachers of these other subjects might be useful; indeed, there could be opportunity for joint projects.

Also the project suggestions have not been written in a uniform style. In some cases we have given mathematical background where it might be unfamiliar; in others we have been briefer. Where possible we have given references, some of which are directly accessible by pupils, and some are at teacher level.

It should be emphasised that the projects are not prescriptive. We have tried to suggest some possible starting points which we hope will spark off other lines of inquiry. Above all, it is the flavour of a project-based approach which we would wish to convey.

List of project topics

Measurement
1 Measuring length
2 Measuring time
3 Measuring reaction times
4 Measuring the cost of living
5 Ergonomics
6 The calendar
7 Weight watching
8 Calculating calories
9 Writing styles and readability tests

Sport
10 Bouncing balls
11 Jumping potential
12 Predicting athletic performance
13 Decathlon and heptathlon
14 Football results
15 Matches, tournaments and timetables
16 Scoring systems

Games and amusements
17 Noughts and crosses
18 Matchstick puzzles
19 Matchstick games
20 Magic squares
21 Tangrams
22 Chessboard contemplations
23 Designing games of chance
24 Mathematical magic
25 Monopoly
26 Snooker
27 Gambling
28 Simulating games on a computer

The home
29 Planning a new kitchen
30 Decorating and furnishing a room
31 Ideal home
32 Moving house
33 DIY secondary double-glazing
34 Loft conversions

1 ▪ Measuring length

Egyptian royal cubit
The cubit of King Amenhotep I 1559–1539 B.C.18th dynasty

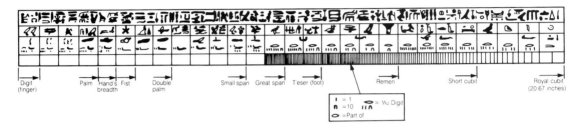

The story of the background to different measurements of length is fascinating. The measures reflect clearly the needs of a society at a given time and a study of them puts our current system into perspective.

1 Body measures

Most systems of measures of length seem to be based on the human body. The Egyptians used:

digit = one finger width
palm = 4 digits
hand = 5 digits
cubit = distance from elbow to finger tip
= 28 digits

The Romans used the length of a foot and a pace, the latter being the distance between the point where a heel leaves the ground and next makes contact. The Roman mile, equal to 1000 paces (*mille passus*), was then used to measure how far their legions marched.

The variation of these units led to the *need for a standard measure* and King Henry I of England, who reigned in the 12th century, decreed that a yard should be the distance from the end of *his* nose to the end of *his* thumb. Later King Edward I had a *standard yard* made from an iron bar and declared that a *foot* would be exactly one-third of its length.

(a) Find out what these units measure on yourself and compare them with some of your friends.

What is the average, and the variation in these measurements?

How would 1000 of your paces compare with a standard mile?

(b) Traditional translations of the Bible give the height of Goliath (1 Sam 17:4), the size of Noah's ark (Gen 6:15) and the depth of the Flood (Gen 7:20) in cubits. Many other biblical measurements are also given in cubits such as details of a variety of buildings for King Solomon (1 Kings 6 and 7), and the length of the city wall destroyed by Jehoash (2 Kings 14:13). Look up these references and convert the measurements into those we now use to get a better understanding of their size. If you have the use of a Bible concordance, you will be able to find many other references to cubits.

(c) The lengths of the human body are closely linked to the imperial units used today. One inch is related to the width of a man's thumb, the foot to the length of a man's foot, and the yard was originally described as the length from the tip of the nose to the end of the thumb of an outstretched arm. Investigate these measurements on a variety of people.

2 Scientific measures

With the development of science there came a greater *need for precision* so by the 19th century the iron bar had been replaced by a special bronze bar whose length at 62°F was taken as a yard. Find out how the units of length are defined even more precisely by the modern scientific community.

As people's range of experiences increased there was a need to extend the range of units they used. For example, astronomers are concerned with very large distances and measure them in *light-years*. They also use *astronomical units* (AU) and *parsecs* (pc). Find out how these units are defined and how they relate to a mile and a kilometre.

At the other extreme are very small units. What is an *angstrom* (Å)? What is it used to measure?

3 The metric system

This system was first suggested by French scientists in about 1790. How did they define a metre? What is the great virtue of the metric system which has seen it adapted very widely and replace the system based on yards, feet and inches?

How small are millimetres, micrometres, nanometres, picometres, femtometres, attometres?

4 Miscellaneous measures

In use not so very long ago, and some in current use, are a variety of units of length with interesting connections. See what you can find out about: a rod, a pole, a perch, a furlong, a chain, a league, a fathom, an ell.

What unit is used to measure the height of a horse?

One definition for a *rod* current in the 16th century was to line up and measure the length of the feet of the first 16 men out of church as they stood toe to heel!

5 Distance as time

Distance is often given in terms of time where a certain mode of travel is assumed such as 'a two hour walk'. Find other examples and explain how time can be a measure of distance.

6 Your own system

Design a system of measures of length and show how it can be used for measuring everyday objects as well as very small and very large distances. Make appropriate measuring devices.

References

Exploring Mathematics on your own: The World of Measurement (John Murray)

Open University, PME233, *Mathematics Across the Curriculum, Unit 3: Measuring* (Open University)

The Diagram Group, *The Book of Comparisons* (Penguin)

L. Hogben, *Man Must Measure* (Rathbone)

T. Smith, *The Story of Measurement* (Blackwell)

Cruden's Complete Concordance to the Old and New Testaments (Lutterworth)

Encyclopaedias

2 ▪ Measuring time

Our lives seem to be ruled by time. Public transport runs to a predetermined timetable, radio and television programmes start at precise times. Being early or late for work or school is all a result of our fixation with time. How and why has the measurement of time developed?

The apparent passage of the sun across the sky was one of the first things to be exploited for the measurement of time. It led to the development of shadow clocks and sundials. The disadvantage of shadow clocks is that they are only of use when the sun is shining. This problem was overcome by the invention of water clocks (clepsydra), candle clocks and sand timers.

Short periods of time are not reliably measured by the above devices. Galileo (1581) is often said to have been the first to recognise the importance of the regular swing of a pendulum as a way of measuring short periods of time. Its use is seen in grandfather clocks, for example, where the pendulum is designed to swing from one side to the other in one second.

1 Using the sun

The movement of the shadow of a stick during the day led to the development of shadow clocks and sundials. Find out what you can about them. Make and calibrate a shadow clock.

Why is the 'gnomon' (the pin or stick) of a sundial set at an angle equal to the latitude of the place where it is being used?

2 Clepsydra, candle clocks and sand timers

Find out what you can about the historical development of these devices. Make and test the accuracy of one or more of them. To help, details of a clepsydra are given below.

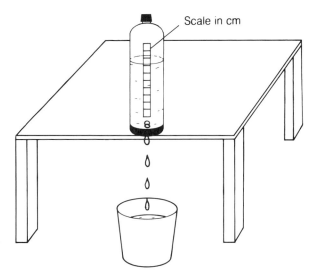

Scale in cm

The water clock is based on measuring the volume of water which drips from a small hole made in the side of a large container. The disadvantage of this method of measuring time is obvious to anyone who has filled a watering can from a tank: as the water level drops the flow decreases. This can lead to an experiment to find how the rate of flow depends on the depth of the water.

Obtain a plastic bottle such as an orange squash bottle. Make a *small* hole in the vertical curved surface, near the bottom. Attach a strip of paper marked in centimetres to the bottom so that the zero is at the level of the hole. Fill the bottle to the highest mark. Record the times for the water level to drop to the marks on the paper strip. Repeat this several times to calculate the mean time for each height. Plot a graph and try to find a relationship between height and time. The bottle could then be calibrated to give time directly.

3 Using a pendulum

Make a simple pendulum by suspending a heavy object on a thread and investigate the time of say 10 swings for different lengths of thread. How does the time vary with (a) the weight, (b) the amplitude of the swing, and (c) the length of the string? What length pendulum is required to make one swing in one second? If one pendulum is four times as long as another, what is the relation between their times of swing?

4 Using periodic events

Any events which occur periodically can be used as a basis of a measurement of time. The phases of the moon are clearly related to our months while the times of high and low tides are very significant to people living on the coast whose livelihood depends on the sea. An individual's resting pulse rate might even be a reasonable measure of short intervals of time.

Investigate these and other suitable events to see their advantages and disadvantages.

5 Variation of time on the earth's surface

How does the time of day differ in different parts of the earth's surface and how are time zones used to compensate for it?

6 Clocks and navigation

Why was the development of clocks motivated by navigation?

7 Clock mechanisms

Investigate the mechanisms of clocks and watches. How does the escapement work? How are the relative speeds of the hands obtained?

8 Computer clock

Devise a computer program which gives a display to simulate a digital clock.

References

Life Science Library: Time (Time Life)
K. Welch, *Time Measurement: An Introductory History* (David and Charles; out of print)
S. Strandh, *Machines: an illustrated history* (Nordbok)
L. Hogben, *Mathematics for the Million* (Pan)

3 ▪ Measuring reaction times

It is often necessary to react rapidly to external stimuli – car drivers might need to brake suddenly, games players often need to move quickly. A project testing reaction times can have a natural interest through the personal challenge and the competitive element.

1 Stop the ruler

A ruler is held close to a wall. The person being tested puts a finger at the zero mark. The ruler is dropped and has to be stopped by the outstretched finger.

Compare different people. Compare left hands and right hands. Compare males and females. Do people improve with practice? Do good gamesplayers do well at this test?

Instead of using the graduations on the ruler, the length scale could be replaced by a time scale. Assuming free fall, the distance travelled in t seconds is approximately $5t^2$ metres. Hence in t hundredths of a second the distance the ruler falls is $1/20t^2$ centimetres. Using this result a strip of paper can be

marked directly in hundredths of a second and then glued to the ruler. A standard 30 cm ruler will give times up to about 24 hundredths of a second.

2 Using a computer

A microcomputer has a built-in timer and this is exploited in many computer games. A less exciting but simpler program can be used to calculate reaction times directly:

```
10 CLS
20 INPUT "How many goes",N
30 FOR I = 1 TO N
40 Z = RND(26) + 64
50 PRINT
60 PRINT "Press the key marked ";
   CHR$(Z)
70 T = TIME
80 REPEAT UNTIL GET = Z
90 PRINT "That took you ";
   (TIME − T)/100; " seconds"
100 NEXT I
```

The program can be extended to calculate the mean reaction time at the end.

Variations to the program can be made.
(a) Find the response time for a specific letter or number. For example, the person being tested has to press the space bar (or any key) when the number 1 appears.
(b) Arrange for a sound to be activated when a certain number is obtained by the random generator. The person has to respond by pressing a key.
(c) Arrange for colours to be flashed onto the screen at random. The person has to respond to yellow, say.

References

Schools Council, *Statistics in Your World: Practice Makes Perfect* (Foulsham Educational)

4 ▪ Measuring the cost of living

The costs of goods and services rarely seem to stand still. Some costs such as bus fares steadily increase, while others such as the cost of fresh fruit and vegetables fluctuate with the seasons. Each month the British government publishes the *retail price index* (RPI) which attempts to put a figure to the general level of prices.

How can a figure be obtained to measure the cost of living at a given time?

To be most effective these projects should be continued over several months.

1 'Shopping baskets'

At times the BBC has popularised the idea of an index to measure the cost of living by considering the basic food requirements for an average family for a week and seeing what they would cost to buy in the shops. This 'shopping basket' approach contains the essential ideas of a cost of living index.

Decide on an average family of say two adults and two children of school age and make a list of their weekly food requirements such as: 12 pints of milk, 500 grams of butter, 5 loaves of bread, 500 grams of cheese, 3 kilograms of potatoes etc. When the contents of the shopping basket has been established their cost is worked out each week and this figure is taken as a measure of the cost of living. This figure's fluctuation over a period of time gives a good guide to the day-to-day cost of living for the average family. It can be illustrated graphically, trends noted and future costs forecast.

2 Local shops or supermarket?

Compare the cost of living for a person using small local shops to a person with access to a supermarket or out-of-town shopping centre.

3 Total household cost of living

Construct a more elaborate model of the cost of living for your family based on other normal expenditure such as transport, heating and lighting, rent, clothing, newspapers etc. in addition to the food. How does it compare with the simpler food basket model?

4 Government RPI

Find out all you can about the government's retail price index.

References

The Spode Group, *Solving Real Problems with Mathematics, Vol. 1* (Cranfield Press)

A.J. Sherlock, *An Introduction to Probability and Statistics* (Arnold)

Schools Council, *Statistics in Your World: Retail Price Index* (Foulsham Educational)

SMP, *New Book 5* (Cambridge University Press)

SMP 11–16, *Book B5* (Cambridge University Press)

5 ▪ Ergonomics

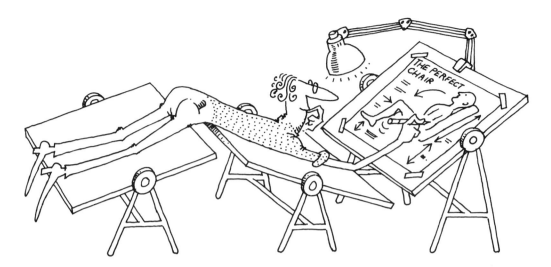

In recent years it has been appreciated that careful design of furniture is needed to ensure the comfort, health and efficiency of people at home and work. There are opportunities here for projects involving measurement and design.

1 Chairs and tables

What is the most comfortable height for a chair for sitting at a table when (a) writing, (b) eating?

What are the best table and chair heights for a typist?

What is the best position for the back support of a chair?

Measure some people – heights of knees and elbows when they are in a sitting position, for example. Check heights of chairs and tables.

2 Kitchens

What is the best height for (a) a working surface, (b) an oven?

What is the most convenient lay-out for a kitchen?

What is the greatest shelf height which can comfortably and safely be reached?

Since low-level cupboards are probably unavoidable, what items should be kept there?

Design a convenient kitchen.

3 Elderly and handicapped people

Many people are likely to have difficulty in reaching and stooping. Visit an elderly or handicapped person and draw up suggestions for improving their home.

4 Cars

Cars are often difficult to get in and out of. Find which models are easiest and, by taking measurements, determine the key factors.

References

The Spode Group, *Solving Real Problems with CSE Mathematics* (Cranfield Press)

6 · The calendar

1 Historical development

- Why do we have 365 days in a year (and one more in leap years)?
- Was 1900 a leap year? Will 2000 be a leap year? Why do we have leap years?
- Why are there 28, 29, 30 or 31 days in a month?
- Why are there 7 days in a week?
- Why is the *tenth* month called October? (Octo- means eight in other contexts.)
- Why does Easter occur at different times?

Questions such as these raise many interesting issues which can lead to a study of the historical development of the calendar.

2 The day for any date

Knowing the day for a given date it is possible to work out the day for any other date. The key idea is that 1st January, say, moves on by one day each year except in a year after a leap year when it moves on by two days.

(a) If you are given the day for 1st January this year, devise a method for finding the day for any other date this year.

(b) Given the day for 1st January this year work out the day for 1st January 1900.

(c) From the day for 1st January 1900 work out a method for determining the day for any other date in the twentieth century.

(d) Write a computer program for your method in (c).

A TABLE TO FIND EASTER DAY

FROM THE PRESENT TIME TILL THE YEAR 2199 INCLUSIVE ACCORDING TO THE FOREGOING CALENDAR

Golden Number	Day of the Month	Sunday Letter
	March 21	C
XIV	— 22	D
III	— 23	E
	— 24	F
XI	— 25	G
	— 26	A
XIX	— 27	B
VIII	— 28	C
	— 29	D
XVI	— 30	E
V	— 31	F
	April 1	G
XIII	— 2	A
II	— 3	B
	— 4	C
X	— 5	D
	— 6	E
XVIII	— 7	F
VII	— 8	G
	— 9	A
XV	— 10	B
IV	— 11	C
	— 12	D
XII	— 13	E
I	— 14	F
	— 15	G
IX	— 16	A
XVII	— 17	B
VI	— 18	C
	— 19	D
	— 20	E
	— 21	F
	— 22	G
	— 23	A
	— 24	B
	— 25	C

THIS Table contains so much of the Calendar as is necessary for the determining of *Easter*; to find which, look for the Golden Number of the year in the first Column of the Table, against which stands the day of the Paschal Full Moon; then look in the third column for the Sunday Letter, next after the day of the Full Moon, and the day of the Month standing against that Sunday Letter is *Easter Day*. If the Full Moon happens upon a Sunday, then (according to the first rule) the next Sunday after is *Easter Day*.

To find the Golden Number, or Prime, add one to the Year of our Lord, and then divide by 19; the remainder, if any, is the Golden Number; but if nothing remaineth, then 19 is the Golden Number.

To find the Dominical or Sunday Letter, according to the Calendar, until the year 2099 inclusive, add to the Year of our Lord its fourth part, omitting fractions; and also the number 6: Divide the sum by 7; and if there is no remainder, then A is the Sunday Letter: But if any number remaineth, then the Letter standing against that number in the small annexed Table is the Sunday Letter.

0	A
1	G
2	F
3	E
4	D
5	C
6	B

For the next following Century, that is, from the year 2100 till the year 2199 inclusive, add to the current year its fourth part, and also the number 5, and then divide by 7, and proceed as in the last Rule.

NOTE, That in all Bissextile or Leap-Years, the Letter found as above will be the Sunday Letter, from the intercalated day exclusive to the end of the year.

lvii

References

Life Science Library: Time (Time Life)

B. Bolt, *More Mathematical Activities* (Cambridge University Press)

Mathematical Association, *132 Short Programs for the Mathematics Classroom* (Mathematical Association)

The Spode Group, *Solving Real Problems with CSE Mathematics* (Cranfield Press)

7 ▪ Weight watching

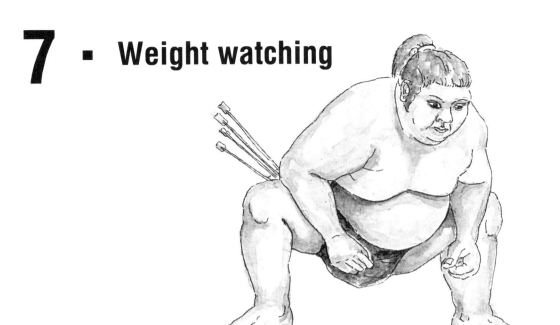

Many people are considered overweight or underweight but this assumes some normal weight. This project looks at average weights and their relationship with a healthy weight.

1 Average weights

To get some idea of what the norm might be for a given age it is necessary to collect a lot of data on heights and weights. This may be available in school records but the organising and recording of these measurements for a particular age group in the school would be a useful part of such a project.

A scatter diagram of weights against heights would then be a good way of representing the data.

Should girls and boys be recorded separately?

What is the average weight? How can the spread be measured? What should be considered a healthy weight for a given height?

Obtain tables giving the normal weights and see how they compare with your findings.

2 The body mass index

The body mass index (BMI) is used as a measure of a person's relative size. It is defined by

$$\text{BMI} = \frac{\text{Mass in kilograms}}{(\text{Height in metres})^2}$$

An American survey has concluded that the healthiest group with the greatest life expectancy is associated with the range 20 to 25. Ballerinas, who are frequently underweight, tend to be outside this range as are the very gross Sumo wrestlers. Use this index to work out a range of weights for people with heights between 1.50 m and 1.90 m.

3 Weight changes from birth

How does a person's weight change with age from the time they are born?

References

Good tables of height/weight/age for boys and girls are to be found in, for example, A.E. Bender, *Calories and Nutrition* (Mitchell Beazley)

8 ▪ Calculating calories

A person's energy input should match their energy output unless they are trying to lose or to gain weight. There are wide variations in people's life styles which require different inputs, as well as variations in the calorific values of food. This project should give some insight towards sensible eating.

The energy potential of food and the energy expended by a person is measured in *calories*. Sugar for example can supply 4 calories of energy per gram, whilst sleeping uses up about 1.1 calories in a minute. This compares with the 10 calories required to boil enough water for one cup of tea.

1 Energy requirements

Use the following information and/or any other similar information you can find to estimate your daily energy expenditure:

Activity	Calories used per minute
sleeping	1.1
washing and dressing	2.8
walking (slowly–quickly)	2.9–5.2
sitting	1.2–1.5
standing	1.6–1.9
light domestic work	3.0
gardening	4.8
cycling (slowly–fast)	4.5–11.0
playing tennis	7.1
playing football	8.9
playing squash	10.0

2 Energy intake

The average recommended daily intake for most healthy adults and teenagers is about 2000 calories for a female and 2700 for a male, but this will vary considerably with a person's occupation.

(a) Find out the calorific values of the foods you eat and drink and see how your daily input matches your requirements. Some examples of the energy in food are:
milk   360 calories/pint
breakfast cereal   100 calories/30 g
roast pork   240 calories/30 g
a standard (size 3) boiled egg
80 calories
a standard scrambled egg   170 calories

(b) Produce a weekly menu to match your requirements. A balanced diet requires much more than balancing calories. To take this further look at books on nutrition.

References

Any good book on diet and nutrition such as A. E. Bender, *Calories and Nutrition* (Mitchell Beazley)
The Diagram Group, *The Book of Comparisons* (Penguin)
Netherhall Software, *Balance Your Diet* (Cambridge University Press)

9 ▪ Writing styles and readability tests

Here are some sweets.

Some are for Peter and some for Jane.

They have some sweets.

They like sweets.

On the other hand once the definition is provided the theorem ceases to be obvious, since the result it asserts is quite different from the defining property and to show that the first follows the second is not a trivial task. If it is objected that we should take as definition some property designed to make the proof simpler, the answer is that there are many other 'obvious' and important properties of continuous functions and no definition simplifies them all simultaneously. We might of course lump together everything we want of a continuous function, and call a function continuous whenever it has these properties. Apart from the crudity and clumsiness of such a procedure, we should thereby entirely obscure the fact that all such properties in fact flow from one simple basic one; we should lose all insight into the relative depths of the properties and into the nature of their interconnections; we might even unwittingly include properties that were subtly inconsistent; and it would take too long to decide whether a given function was continuous.

Some books are easy to read; others are heavy-going, even though their subject content might not be advanced. Is it possible to compare writing styles mathematically and to measure 'readability'?

1 Lengths of words and sentences

(a) Simple books often have short words. One method of comparison might be to compare the lengths of words. Try it out with two contrasting books. Select some pages at random. Find the mean word length for each book.

Draw bar charts (with appropriate groupings).

Compare the word lengths in two novels by different authors.

Does an author, such as Thomas Hardy, have a consistent mean word length?

(b) A second method of comparison might be through sentence lengths. Carry out some comparisons as in (a).

Given some passages from a novel could the author be deduced by consideration of the sentence lengths?

2 Frequency of common words

A biblical scholar, A. Q. Morton, investigated the authorship of the epistles in the New Testament. Using the Greek versions he counted the frequency of use of some common words such as *kai* (and), *de* (but), *en* (in). He came to the conclusion that Galatians, Romans, 1st and 2nd Corinthians were probably all written by the same person (St Paul?) and that the other epistles were possibly written by a variety of other people.

Carry out a similar test of authorship on some novels.

3 Readability tests

Teachers and psychologists have devised tests to determine how easy it is to read a book. One of the first tests was the Reading Ease (RE) formula due to Flesch (1948):

$$RE = 206.835 - 0.846S - 1.015W$$

where S is the average number of syllables per 100 words and W is the average number of words per sentence. 'Reading Ease' is an index whose value can range from 0 to 100 (incomprehensible to transparently easy).

A second method, which is easier to use, is the FOG formula (Gunning 1952):

$$F = 0.4(W + P)$$

where W is the average number of words per sentence and P is the percentage of words containing three or more syllables (excluding those ending in *-ed* or *-ing*). FOG stands for 'frequency of gobbledygook'.

A further measure is the SMOG formula (simple measure of gobbledygook; McLaughlin 1969). Select 10 consecutive sentences near the beginning, 10 near the middle and 10 near the end of the book. Count the number n of words with three or more syllables. The SMOG grade is $3 + \sqrt{n}$.

The FOG and SMOG formulae give grade levels on the American school system; add 5 to obtain the UK reading level/age.

Apply these tests to some books.

4 Primary school reading schemes

Compare the language in various reading schemes used in primary schools.

References

J. Gilliland, *Readability* (University of London Press)

H. Shuard and A. Rothery (eds.), *Children Reading Mathematics* (Murray)

C. Harrison, *Readability in the Classroom* (Cambridge University Press)

10 ▪ Bouncing balls

Everyone has played or watched a variety of ball games such as tennis, football, golf, basket-ball, and squash. In all these games the bounce of the ball off the playing surface or striking implement is very important. For this reason manufacturers have to make balls whose bounce meets standards set down by each game's organising body. The object of this project is to see how to measure the bounce of a ball and to compare its performance and that of other balls under varying conditions.

The agreed regulations for a ball are usually given by stating the height to which it must bounce off a specific surface when dropped from a known height. A tennis ball, for example, when dropped from a height of 200 cm onto a concrete surface, should bounce to between 106 cm and 116 cm. The activities here use this method to compare the bounce of a variety of balls under varying conditions.

1 The bounce of a tennis ball

(a) Obtain a tennis ball and measure the height (h cm) to which it bounces when dropped from a variety of heights (H cm) from say 1 metre to 5 metres onto a concrete surface. Draw a graph of h against H. What do you conclude?

What precautions did you take to ensure the measure of the height of the bounce was accurate?

(b) Tennis is not played on a concrete surface. Carry out experiments to see how the bounce would differ off (i) grass, (ii) clay, (iii) wooden surfaces. How does this different bounce affect the game?

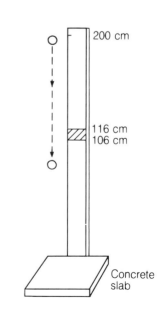

200 cm

116 cm
106 cm

Concrete slab

2 Comparing the bounce of different kinds of ball

Obtain a golf ball and a basket ball (or other large ball) and investigate their bounce in the same way.

Which ball bounces best off concrete, and which off grass? Does the relative order of the balls' bouncinesses stay the same for all surfaces?

3 Variation of bounce with temperature

The bounce of some balls changes significantly with temperature. A squash ball has very little bounce until it is 'warmed up'. One way to control the temperature of a ball for an experiment would be to hold it under water heated to a known temperature before testing its bounce.

Investigate the way in which the bounce of a squash ball and a table-tennis ball vary with temperature. A fridge could be used to produce low temperatures but be wary of the warmth of your hand on the ball before you bounce it.

4 Bounce off a racket

How well does a tennis ball bounce off a racket? Clamp a racket and then drop a ball from a height onto it. Investigate the effect of (a) different kinds of stringing, (b) different string tensions, (c) different parts of the face of the racket.

5 Lengths of successive bounces

Take a ball and bounce it across the floor, noting where it lands at each bounce. (One way to do this is to wet the ball so that it leaves a mark at each point of contact with the floor.) Measure the length of each bounce and calculate the ratio of successive lengths. This ratio is constant and gives another way of measuring the bounce of a ball.

(N.B. The square of this ratio should equal the ratio of the heights of successive bounces for the same ball dropped vertically onto the same surface.)

6 Specifications for different balls

Try to find the regulations which apply to different kinds of ball.

References

B. Bolt, *Even More Mathematical Activities*, Activity 91 (Cambridge University Press)

C. B. Daish, *The Physics of Ball Games* (English Universities Press)

11 • Jumping potential

The standing broad jump

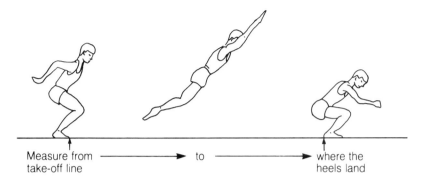

Measure from take-off line →→ to →→ where the heels land

It can take many years to develop a good high jump or long jump technique, but it is possible to do a simple experiment to test a person's spring and go some way to predicting their potential. The idea of this project is to test the springs of a group of people and then to see how well the results correlate with their abilities in different jumping events.

In carrying out the following tests, it is more reliable to allow each person to do each test three times and to record their best effort.

1 The vertical jump test

The simplest measure of a person's spring is their ability to leap vertically.

In this test a person stands facing a wall with heels on the ground and arms reaching upwards to their full extent. The point where the tip of their outstretched fingers touch the wall is noted. The person now leaps vertically in the air to touch the wall as high as possible, and the point where the fingers reach is again noted. The difference in height between the points where the fingers touch is then recorded as a measure of the jump.

This test should be carried out with a minimum of 20 people, ideally with a considerable range of physical abilities, and the results carefully recorded.

2 The standing broad jump

The standing broad jump makes use of the same muscle groups as the vertical jump so it is a reasonable hypothesis that the performance in the two events should be correlated.

In the broad jump a person stands with their toes against a take-off line, swings their arms, bends their legs and leaps as far as possible across the ground. The distance from the take-off line to where their heels first meet the ground on landing is recorded as the measure of the jump.

The people who were tested for the vertical jump should now be measured for their ability at broad jumping and the results recorded.

3 Comparing the broad jump with the vertical jump

On a graph which shows 'length of broad jump' along the x-axis and 'length of vertical jump' up the y-axis, put a small cross to represent each of the people tested. It should be found that these crosses lie approximately on a straight line. Draw in the best straight line you can. What is the equation of the line? What physical characteristics do people have whose crosses lie above the line?

4 Predicting a person's ability to broad jump

Measure the vertical jump of a new person and use your graph to try to predict their likely ability to broad jump. Now get the person to broad jump. How good was the prediction?

5 Comparing the triple jump with the vertical jump

Investigate the possible relation between a person's ability to do a vertical jump and their ability to do a *standing* hop, step and jump.

(Note that the *standing* start is suggested because a running start brings in the additional factor of a person's sprinting potential, which confuses the issue.)

6 How do physical characteristics affect jumping potential?

The relative weights of different people of the same height will influence their ability to do a vertical jump. The relative length of a person's leg to height and, even more, the relative lengths of each part of the leg are also significant.

By obtaining the vertical jumps of a number of people with approximately the same height, see what you can find about the relationship between their physical characteristics and jumping potential.

Standing start

Hop   Step   Jump

Measure from take-off line → to → where the heels land

Hop, step and jump

References

W. R. Campbell and N. M. Tucker, *An Introduction to Tests and Measurement in Physical Education* (Bell)

B. L. Johnson and J. K. Nelson, *Practical Measurements for Evaluation in Physical Education* (Burgess)

M. J. Haskins, *Evaluation in Physical Education* (W. C. Brown)

12 ▪ Predicting athletic performance

From known performances in athletic events it is possible to predict with considerable accuracy the likely performances in related events.

1 Women's world track records

Distance	Time	Average speed
100 metres	10.76	9.3 ms^{-1}
200 metres	21.71	9.2 ms^{-1}
400 metres	47.60	8.4 ms^{-1}
800 metres	1:53.28	7.1 ms^{-1}
1500 metres	3:52.47	6.45 ms^{-1}

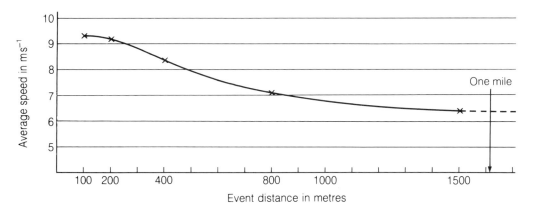

As an example of the possibilities, above are given the women's world track records of five distances from 100 m to 1500 m as they stood at the end of 1987. An average running speed has been calculated for each distance and these have then been plotted on a graph. Only the crosses on the graph represent real data but it is possible to join these by a smooth curve and predict the likely average running speed for intermediate distances.

(a) Make an accurate drawing of the above graph to find the average speed predicted for a 1000 m world record and hence the likely time for such an event. How does your answer compare with the actual record of 2:30.6?

(b) Draw a graph showing distance against time taken (convert minutes to seconds). Use the graph to predict the world record mile time (4:15.8). Try to extend the graph to predict the 2000 m, 3000 m, 5000 m and 10 000 m records (these were 5:28.72, 8:22.62, 14:58.89 and 30:59.42 respectively).

(c) Make a similar analysis of men's world track records.

(d) Analyse your school records and various age group records and see if the same shape graph emerges.

2 World mile records for men

Year	Athlete	Time	Time (in seconds)
1913	John Jones, USA	4:14.4	254
1923	Paavo Nurmi, Finland	4:10.4	250
1933	Jack Lovelock, New Zealand	4:07.6	248
1943	Arne Andersson, Sweden	4:02.6	243
1954	Roger Bannister, Great Britain	3:59.4	239
1964	Peter Snell, New Zealand	3:54.1	234
1975	Filbert Bayi, Tanzania	3:51.0	231
1985	Steve Cram, Great Britain	3:46.3	226

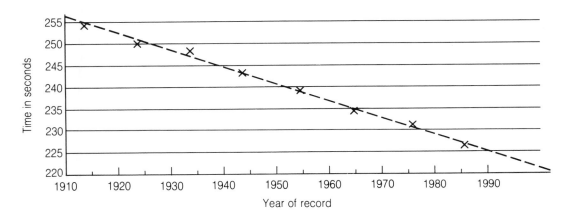

An interesting study of athletic events is to see how world records have improved with time. A good example of this is given by a selection of the world mile records for men shown above. Taken at approximately 10 yearly intervals the records seem to all fit very closely to a linear relationship which is illustrated graphically.

(a) Find the other occasions on which the record was broken this century and see where they would come on the graph.

(b) What does the graph predict for the mile record in 1995? When would you first expect to see the mile run in 3:40?

(c) Analyse the records over time of other events and try to predict future records. With some events there have been quantum leaps due to improved equipment such as in the pole vault or new techniques such as the high jump. What else influences records?

References

Peter Matthews, *Guinness Track and Field Athletics – the records* (Guinness Superlatives)
Peter Matthews (ed.), *Athletics: the International Track and Field Annual* (Simon and Schuster)
The Spode Group, *Solving Real Problems with Mathematics, Vol. 1* (Cranfield Press)

13 ▪ Decathlon and heptathlon

The decathlon and heptathlon are the ultimate events staged to determine the best athletes. With their mixed disciplines of running, hurdling, throwing and jumping the competitors are tested against a set of standards. Depending on how far they fall short of or exceed these standards they are awarded less than or more than 1000 points. The points awarded for each discipline are then added together and the athlete with the highest total wins. To make these competitions fair the 1000 point standard must represent the same level of performance in each event. How can this be achieved? How are the points awarded to the other levels of performance arrived at?

1 International events

Britain has two of the leading exponents:
Daley Thompson holds the decathlon world record of 8847 points:

  100 m, long jump, shot, high jump, 400 m, 110 m hurdles, discus, polevault, javelin, 1500 m

Judy Simpson holds the heptathlon Commonwealth record of 6282 points:

  100 m hurdles, high jump, shot, 200 m, long jump, javelin, 800 m.

Find the level of performance in each event which corresponds to 1000 points. How many points would the current world records in these events be worth?

What were the individual performances which Daley Thompson achieved to get the world decathlon record? What did they each score in points? Daley's personal goal is to exceed 9000 points. Which discipline shows most room for improvement?

How did Judy achieve her Commonwealth record in 1986?

2 School events

(a) Make up a pentathlon of running, jumping and throwing events for your own age group. Take the school's age group athletic records as your standard or some other measure which you think gives the same level of performance in each of the five disciplines you choose and award that 100 points. Now decide what performance is worth 80, 90 . . . 110 points. You may find the PE staff have books of standards which will help you in this task.

(b) Organise a pentathlon based on your model. See if you can use a microcomputer to compute and record the results.

References

Peter Matthews, *Guinness Track and Field Athletics – the records* (Guinness Superlatives)
Peter Matthews (ed.), *Athletics: the International Track and Field Annual* (Simon and Schuster)
IAAF, *Scoring Tables for Men's and Women's Combined Event Competitions* (International Amateur Athletic Federation)
D. Couling, *The AAA Esso Five Star Award Scheme Scoring Tables* (D. Couling, 102 High Street, Castle Donnington, Derby)
N. Dickinson, *English Schools Athletic Association Handbook* (N. Dickinson, 26 Coniscliffe Road, Stanley, Co Durham, DH9 7RF)
The Guinness Book of Records (Guinness Superlatives)

14 ▪ Football results

The game of football is a source of interest to many pupils. Here are some possible topics for research which could be investigated for national results or for school teams. Many pupils are likely to have questions of their own which they would wish to follow up. Some of the questions could be used as on-going projects during the football season. The data required is readily available in newspapers, or, alternatively, previous years' results are available from the football annuals listed in the references.

1 Are football teams more likely to win at home?

2 Does the number of home wins, score draws, non-score draws vary much each week?

3 How variable are football scores?

4 How variable is the mean score of the teams in a league each week?

5 How variable is the difference between scores, i.e. (score of winning team) − (score of losing team)?

6 Is there much difference in the scores in each division? For example, do teams in the First Division score more goals than teams in the Fourth Division?

7 Compare English and Scottish results.

8 Is there a relationship between goals for and goals against?

9 How much movement is there in a league table? Do teams which are in the bottom part of the table early in the season stay there?

10 Does attendance depend on the position in the league table?

11 Have football attendances declined over the years?

12 Have there been changes in the mean scores, variability of scores, etc. over the years?

13 What would be the effect of changing the points scheme? Before 1981 in England two points were awarded for a win and one for a draw. Subsequently three points have been given for a win, and one for a draw. A computer program could be devised to allow various points schemes to be tested.

14 How good are newspapers at predicting football results? Can you devise a method for predicting next week's results? Compare your method with a method based on random numbers.

15 A striking way to represent football results is to use a three-dimensional bar chart showing home scores and away scores. As part of the project pupils could make their own cubes from card using an appropriate net.

For example, a score of Arsenal 4 Everton 0 is represented by a cube with 'co-ordinates' (4, 0).

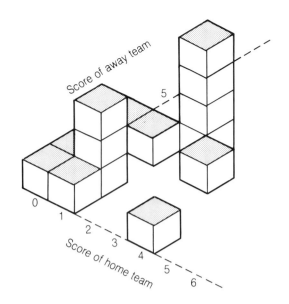

References

Rothman's Football Yearbook (Queen Anne Press)
Playfair Football Annual (Queen Anne Press)
Football League Tables (Collins)
Schools Council, *Statistics in Your World: On the Ball* (Foulsham Educational)
News of the World Football Yearbook

15 · Matches, tournaments and timetables

The need to devise schedules for competitions arises frequently wherever games are played. PE teachers at school might welcome some assistance. Problems of scheduling also arise in school timetabling.

1 League competitions

In a league competition each team has to play every other team once at home and away. Devise schedules for various numbers of teams.

Two possible devices for solving the problem are (a) a rotating disc, and (b) a box of cubes.

(a) Suppose there are eight teams A, B, C, D, E, F, G and H. Mark seven equally-spaced points around a circle. On a piece of acetate draw the lines shown and fix the acetate with a pin through the centre of the circle.

Then the matches for the first week are A–H, B–G, C–F, D–E.

By rotating the acetate the matches for the subsequent weeks can be read off.

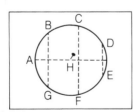

(b) Label eight cubes A, B, C, D, E, F, G, H and put them in a box as shown on the right. The pairs A–H, B–G, C–F and D–E give the matches for the first week.

Remove H, move A down, slide the top row to the left, move E up, slide the bottom row to the right and replace H.

The new pairs give the matches for the second week. Continue the procedure.

(c) How can these methods be adapted for an odd number of teams?

2 Knockout competitions

In knockout competitions (such as the national Football Cup) teams are eliminated at each round. How many games are played in each round? What happens when there is an odd number of teams? How many teams will have a bye in the first round?

3 Speedway competitions

In speedway competitions heats involve four riders, and every rider has to compete against every other rider. Devise schedules.

4 Timetables

How are the subject blocks chosen in the options scheme for the school timetable? What problems arise in staffing and rooming? Genuine problems could be given to pupils to solve.

References

M. Kraitchik, *Mathematical Recreations* (Allen and Unwin)

B. Bolt, *Even More Mathematical Activities*, activities 44, 58, 108 (Cambridge University Press)

16 ▪ Scoring systems

Most people who watch or play sport have had occasion to reflect on the result of a match and wonder whether the scoring system had brought about a fair result. An analysis of a selection of scoring systems showing their strengths and weaknesses and giving reasoned alternatives would make an interesting project.

1 Racket games

In most racket games the loser can have scored more points than the winner. A squash player who loses 9–0, 9–0, 9–10, 9–10, 9–10 may feel hard done by, having scored 45 points to the opponent's 30. How unbalanced can the scores become in tennis, or badminton, or table tennis? Can you suggest alternative systems which are fairer?

2 Cricket

In cricket it is the total number of runs which matter at the end of the match for short matches, but the longer matches so often end in unsatisfactory draws. Can you suggest a better alternative?

3 Football

Football matches are frequently low scoring and depend on chance goals against the run of play. How could corners and free kicks, for example, be used in a scheme to produce a fairer result?

In the football league how might away success be better awarded?

4 Rugby

Rugby has a points scheme which takes more into account than the tries but is too dominated by the skills of the goal kicker. How might the points scheme be modified to improve the situation? Propose a scheme and see how it would work out in specific matches.

5 Tariff systems

Diving and gymnastic competitions use a tariff system to weight the points which take into account the difficulty of what the competitor attempts. Investigate these.

6 Athletics

Athletic standards at school are usually related to age. Show how a better system might be devised based on height and weight.

7 Weight-lifting

How would you compare the merits of two weight-lifters of different weights? The *Superstars* competition uses

$$(\text{actual lift}) - (\text{body weight})$$

to measure a person's performance. Contrast this with

$$\frac{\text{actual lift}}{\text{body weight}}$$

and the method used by the Olympic panel of

$$\frac{\text{actual lift}}{(\text{body weight} - 35)^{1/3}}$$

All the weights are in kilograms.

8 Miscellaneous

Investigate scoring systems in golf, show-jumping, boxing, cross-country running, basketball, rifle-shooting, decathlon, etc.

17 · Noughts and crosses

Noughts and crosses is a game with a long history and is played worldwide. It looks easy but one has to think clearly to avoid defeat. However, a player who has analysed and understood the game should never lose. The analysis of this and related games, together with the invention of new versions, gives plenty of scope for an interesting project.

1 Ordinary noughts and crosses

(a) How many ways can a line of three Xs be put on a board? How many lines are controlled by an X in (i) the centre, (ii) the corner, (iii) the middle of a side?

   What is the smallest number of Xs which could block all the possible lines so preventing O winning?

   How many ways can you mark three Xs on the board so that they form two lines each containing two Xs? Why is this kind of arrangement important?

   Analyse the game carefully and explain what moves to make in any situation to avoid defeat.

(b) An interesting version of the normal game is to play so that the first person to get three in a line is the loser. This time the second player is at an advantage but the first player can always make certain of a draw.

2 Three men's morris

The older Chinese and Greek version was often played with six counters, three for each player. The game starts just as usual until all six counters are on the board then players take it in turn to move one of their counters one square up or down or sideways until a player achieves a line.

   This game was also played in medieval England, where it was called 'Three men's morris'. Analyse the strategies involved.

3 Four in a line

Try playing noughts and crosses on a 4 × 4 board; the winner has to get four in a line. Such games are likely to end in a draw for it only takes four Os (or Xs) suitably placed to block all the 10 possible lines. One arrangement is shown here. What others are possible?

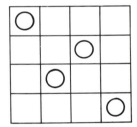

   Playing to find four in a line with a 5 × 5 board is more interesting. Investigate.

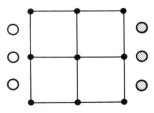

4 Form a square

An interesting version of noughts and crosses is possible on a 4 × 4 or a 5 × 5 board if instead of trying to make a line the players aim to make a square.

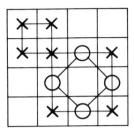

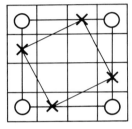

On a 5 × 5 board there are 50 possible squares. Can you find them all? How many squares can be found using a corner square?

What strategy can be used to win this game?

5 Commercial two- and three-dimensional versions

A variety of commercial versions of noughts and crosses are marketed. 'Connect Four' is a two-dimensional version while 'Four Fours' and 'Space Lines' are three-dimensional versions which are interesting to analyse. See, for example, Bolt, *EMMA*, activities 1 and 17.

6 Structurally identical games

There are a family of games which appear quite different from noughts and crosses, but which are structurally identical. For example, take the ace (= 1), 2, 3, . . ., 9 of diamonds from a pack of cards, and place them face up on a table. Two players pick up a card in turn, the aim being to be the first person to have three cards in their hand which total 15.

See Bolt, *EMMA*, activity 54 for other examples. Explain why they are structurally the same. Invent further examples.

7 Invent a game

Invent a new version of noughts and crosses. See Bolt, *MA*, activities 56 and 95.

References

B. Bolt, *Mathematical Activities (MA)* and *Even More Mathematical Activities (EMMA)* (Cambridge University Press)

M. Gardner, *Mathematical Carnival* and *Mathematical Puzzles and Diversions* (Penguin)

18 • Matchstick puzzles

Remove three matches to leave just three identical squares.

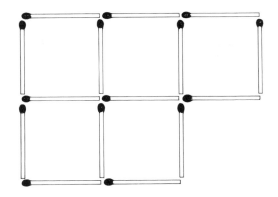

The matchstick puzzle shown here is typical of a large number of similar puzzles which need luck or careful analysis to solve. Developing a strategy for solving these puzzles and describing the strategy with applications to specific examples would make an interesting project involving spatial perception and logical thinking.

1 Words are important!

Solve the puzzle (see *MA*, activity 20). The wording of the puzzle is important. *Remove three matches*, *leave three identical squares*, should all say something to the puzzler.
(a) How many matches will be left when three are removed? Can you tell from the number of matches remaining whether the squares will have any sides in common?
(b) How many ways could you have removed four matches to leave just three identical squares? This time two squares must share a side.
(c) Show how to move four matches to make just three squares. Notice the change from *remove* to *move* and the absence of the word *identical*.

2 Lateral thinking required

(a) The twelve matchsticks arranged as a hexagonal wheel form six identical equilateral triangles. It takes some lateral thinking and a leap into three dimensions to show how they could be rearranged to form eight identical equilateral triangles. (Two solutions are possible!)
(b) Show how to move four of the matches to form three equilateral triangles.

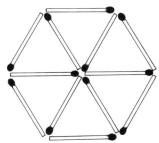

References

B. Bolt, *Mathematical Activities (MA)*, *More Mathematical Activities*, and *Even More Mathematical Activities* (Cambridge University Press)
M. Brooke, *Tricks, Games and Puzzles with Matches* (Dover)
P. Van Delft and J. Botermans, *Creative Puzzles of the World* (Cassell)

19 · Matchstick games

There are a number of games in which matchsticks can be used as counters. Below are descriptions of some of these games, together with suggestions for their analysis and the determination of strategies.

1 Last match loser

This is a game for two players.

Make a pile of 21 matches (or any simple objects like coins or counters). The players take turns to remove matches from the pile. At each turn a player must take at least one match but not more than 4 matches. The player who takes the last match wins.

(a) A strategy can be found by working 'backwards': in order to win you must leave your opponent 5 matches so that if they take 1 or 2 or 3 or 4 matches you take 4 or 3 or 2 or 1. In the same way it can be seen that at the previous stage you must leave 10 matches. Thus certain key numbers can be deduced.
(b) Is it best to go first or second?
(c) Try a different number of matches in the pile.
(d) Change the maximum number of matches which can be taken.
(e) Work out a strategy for N matches where you can take up to n matches at a time.
(f) Change the rules to last player loses.
(g) Write a computer program to play the game.
See *MMA*, activity 68.

2 The game of Nim

In this game there can be more than one pile and any number of matches in each pile, for example, 3, 4, 5.

At each turn a player can take as many matches as desired from one pile only. The last player to go wins.

As in the 'Last match loser', the method is to force your opponent into a key position. Then, no matter what move is made, you can get to another key position.

There is a surprising method for finding key positions: write the number of matches in each pile as a binary number, add up the columns without carrying, make a move so that each column sum will be even.

For example,
$$
\begin{array}{r}
3 \to 11 \\
4 \to 100 \\
5 \to \underline{101} \\
212
\end{array}
$$

Taking two matches from the first pile would make the centre column total even. The first player will then have forced the opponent into a key position.

(a) Find some key positions for 3 piles with up to 10 matches in each pile.
(b) Explain why the method works.
(c) Try other numbers of piles.
(d) Change the rules so that the last player loses.
(e) Harder! Write a computer program for the game.

See *MA*, activity 154.

3 Tsyanshidzi (or Wythoff's Game)

This ancient Chinese game is for two players with two piles of matchsticks (or counters). Each player can either take any number of matches from one pile or an equal number from both piles. The player taking the last match wins.

(a) Again the game depends on key positions which can be found by working backwards from $(0, 0)$.
(b) There is an interesting connection between the numbers for the key positions and the golden ratio (the limit of the ratio of successive terms of a Fibonacci sequence).

See *EMMA*, activity 27.

References

W. W. Rouse Ball, *Mathematical Recreations and Essays* (Macmillan)

B. Bolt, *Mathematical Activities (MA)*, *More Mathematical Activities (MMA)*, and *Even More Mathematical Activities (EMMA)* (Cambridge University Press)

T. H. O'Beirne, *Puzzles and Paradoxes* (Oxford University Press)

M. Gardner, *Mathematical Puzzles and Diversions* (Penguin)

20 ■ Magic squares

3	16	9	22	15
20	8	21	14	2
7	25	13	1	19
24	12	5	18	6
11	4	7	10	23

Bachet de Méziriac's construction

Magic squares have fascinated people of all ages and civilisations for thousands of years. The analysis of known squares and the search for new ones gives insights into mathematics at almost any level. A rich source for many interesting projects.

1 3 × 3 magic squares

There is only one way in which the numbers 1, 2, . . ., 9 can be made into a magic square, but using other sets of numbers there is no end to the squares which can be made. However it is always true that the magic total will be *three* times the number in the middle square. Use this fact to find magic squares of your own.

Can you find magic squares where (a) some numbers are the same, (b) some numbers are negative, (c) some numbers are fractions? A real challenge is to find a square where all the numbers are prime.

2 Constructing magic squares of odd orders

Investigate the *staircase* method for constructing magic squares of odd order devised by Bachet de Méziriac and illustrated above with a 5 × 5 square. How is the magic total related to the centre number?

3 The properties of 4 × 4 magic squares

There are 880 different 4 × 4 magic squares using the numbers 1, 2, 3, . . ., 16. Investigate ways of constructing some of these and then investigate the properties.

See what you can find about Dudeney's classification of these squares into simple, nasik and diabolic.

4 History

See what you can find out about the history of magic squares.

References

B. Bolt, *Mathematical Activities*, and *More Mathematical Activities* (Cambridge University Press)

L. Mottershead, *Sources of Mathematical Discovery* (Blackwell)

M. Gardner, *More Mathematical Puzzles and Diversions* (Penguin)

P. Van Delft and J. Botermans, *Creative Puzzles of the World* (Cassell)

W. S. Andrews, *Magic Squares and Cubes* (Dover)

W. W. Rouse Ball, *Mathematical Recreations and Essays* (Macmillan)

H. E. Dudeney, *Amusements in Mathematics* (Dover)

21 ▪ Tangrams

Tangrams are moving piece or dissection puzzles of ancient Chinese origin which first became popular in Europe and America in the early nineteenth century and have remained popular ever since. An investigation into the various tangrams and the shapes made from them could be the basis of an enjoyable and creative geometric project.

1 Make an accurate drawing of the seven piece tangram square shown here on a piece of thick card. Cut out the pieces and rearrange them to form the hen and the head silhouetted. In each case all the pieces must be used and no overlaps are allowed.

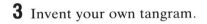

Many other shapes can be made using all seven pieces. See what you can make.

2 Find a source of other tangrams (see the references below) and make your own sets to investigate the shapes which can be made from them. Make accurate drawings of the shapes, and their solution into the tangram pieces.

Two more tangrams are shown here.

3 Invent your own tangram.

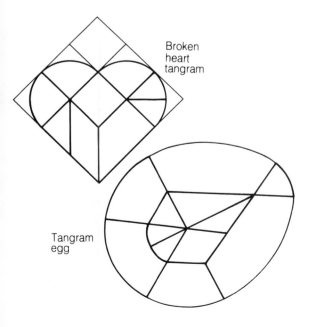

Broken heart tangram

Tangram egg

References

The Mathematical Association produces a 'Tangram Tree' poster, tangram puzzlecards, and pull-apart tangram squares.

P. Van Delft and J. Botermans, *Creative Puzzles of the World* (Cassell)

R. C. Reed, *Tangram: 330 Puzzles* (Tarquin)

K. Saunders, *Hexagrams* (Tarquin)

H. Lindgren, *Recreational Problems in Geometric Dissections and How to Solve Them* (Dover)

J. Elfers, *Tangram: the Ancient Chinese Shapes Game* (Penguin)

B. Bolt, *Even More Mathematical Activities* (Cambridge University Press)

22 ▪ Chessboard contemplations

♞	16	13	20	3	18
12	21	2	17	14	27
35	8	15	28	19	4
22	11	34	31	26	29
7	**36**	9	24	5	32
10	23	6	33	30	25

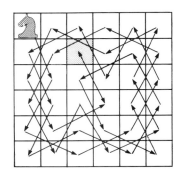

There are many interesting puzzles and recreations associated with the way in which the chess pieces can move on a chessboard. The four projects detailed below are quite independent of each other, but each have their intrinsic interest. They do not depend on knowing how to play chess, but do require a knowledge of how each piece can move.

1 Chessboard tours

(a) *Knight's tours* on a chessboard could form a project on their own. The diagrams show two solutions on a 6 × 6 board and at the same time two ways of recording a solution. The second solution is said to be re-entrant as it ends a knight's move from where it started.
  (i) Find knight's tours on 5 × 5, 7 × 7 and 8 × 8 boards.
  (ii) A knight's tour cannot be completed on a 4 × 4 board. What is the largest number of squares which can be visited without revisiting a square?
  (iii) What is the smallest rectangle on which a tour is possible?
  (iv) Investigate tours on other shapes. (See *MA*, activity 89, and *MMA*, activity 14.)
(b) Investigate tours by rooks, bishops and queens on a chessboard (see Bolt, *MMA*, activity 22).

2 Controlling every square

Investigate the smallest number of knights which can be placed on an $n \times n$ board so that every square is occupied or attacked. Do the same for the other chess pieces. (See Bolt, *MA*, activities 49 and 70.)

3 Avoid three in a line

What is the largest number of pawns which can be put on a chessboard so that no three pawns are in a straight line? (See Bolt, *MA*, activities 1, 2, 3.)

4 Chessboard puzzles

Investigate puzzles involving a chessboard and pieces such as Bolt, *MMA*, activity 24, and *MA*, activity 32.

References

B. Bolt, *Mathematical Activities (MA)*, and *More Mathematical Activities (MMA)* (Cambridge University Press)

W. W. Rouse Ball, *Mathematical Recreations and Essays* (Macmillan)

L. Mottershead, *Sources of Mathematical Discovery* (Blackwell)

23 ▪ Designing games of chance

The aim is to design, analyse and test a game of chance for use at a school fair. A project such as this gives an opportunity for simple ideas of probability to be put to use.

1 Throwing dice

The customer pays 10p a go. You throw two dice and add the top numbers. On some scores the customer wins, on others they lose.

The game can be analysed theoretically from expected frequencies by considering the 36 possible outcomes. With the scheme shown you would expect to pay out 30p on two results, 20p on four results and 10p on six results. This gives a profit of £1.60 on average for every 36 customers. This does not mean that a profit is guaranteed every 36 customers, but in the long run you should win.

Try the game with the pay-out scheme shown. Keep a record of the outcomes so that you can compare your results with the theoretical predictions. Then invent a different pay-out scheme. Analyse it theoretically and try it out. Compare your scheme with the one shown. Which looks most attractive?

2 A marble maze

The customer pays 10p a time to drop a marble in at the top of the board.

The board can be made from plywood. The distances between the nails depend on the diameter of the marbles. The channels at the bottom can be made by glueing strips of wood to the board.

The game can be analysed by considering the theoretical outcomes of dropping 32 marbles in at the top. With the scheme shown this gives a profit of 60p every 32 games.

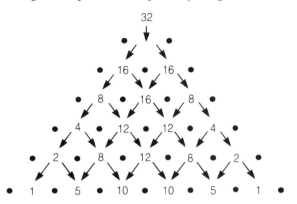

Try the game out as in the last paragraph of 1 above.

3 Rolling coins

The customer pays 10p a go to roll a coin onto a grid of squares, winning 20p if the coin does not lie across a line when it stops.

When the side of the squares is twice the diameter of the coin a consideration of areas shows that the coin would be expected not to finish across a line on a quarter of the goes. So in every 4 goes the expected profit is 20p.

The coin roller can be made from a triangle of wood with a slot cut in it, or alternatively from a folded piece of thick card.

Try the game out as in the last paragraph of 1 above. Invent some variations: for example,
- change the size of the squares,
- have some coloured squares on which the payment is different,
- use a different type of grid (what other shapes tessellate?).

References

Many standard exercises from textbooks can be adapted as games. For example: SMP *Book G*, chapter 3; SMP11–16 *Book Y2*, chapter 17; SMP11–16 *Book B2*, chapter 14 (Cambridge University Press)

4 Cards

The customer pays 10p to pick two cards from a shuffled pack. To win the customer must get
either   two cards of the same suit
or   two cards of the same denomination (for example two sixes)

Work out the theoretical profit for this scheme and try it out.

Design, analyse and try out a pay-out scheme with different numbers for the two ways of winning.

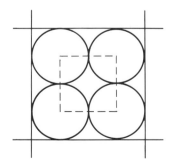

24 · Mathematical magic

Conjuring tricks have a fascination for many people. A number of tricks depend on mathematical principles. Some children might be interested in exploring these ideas and explaining the 'magic'. Some typical examples are given below. Books by Martin Gardner are an excellent source of tricks.

1 Number tricks

$$
\begin{array}{r}
7572 \\
-\ 2757 \\
\hline
4815 \\
\end{array}
$$

$$4 + 1 + 5 = 10$$

Ask someone to write down a telephone number (or any other number – no restriction on the number of digits). They then have to write it down again but with the digits 'scrambled', and subtract the smaller from the larger. They cross out any digit in the result and tell you the sum of the other digits. You can immediately tell which number was deleted.

Method: subtract the total you are given from the next highest multiple of 9. In the example above: $18 - 10 = 8$. (There is a slight problem when the total is a multiple of 9.)

Explain why the trick works.

There are many other tricks which depend on the properties of 9 in the base ten number system.

2 Calendar tricks

July					
Sun.	1	8	15	22	29
Mon.	2	9	16	23	30
Tue.	3	10	17	24	31
Wed.	4	11	18	25	
Thur.	5	12	19	26	
Fri.	6	13	20	27	
Sat.	7	14	21	28	

Ask someone to put a ring round a block of nine numbers on a calendar and tell you the lowest one. You immediately write a number on a piece of paper and ask them to add up the nine numbers in the block. The number you write proves to be the correct total.

Method: add 8 to the lowest number and multiply by 9.

Explain why it works.

Other possibilities:
(a) Ask someone to put a ring round three numbers in a row on a calendar. Given the total you can say what the numbers are.
(b) As in (a) but for a *column* of three numbers.
(c) As in (a) but for a square block of four numbers.
(d) Invent variations with other blocks of numbers.

3 Card tricks

From a pack of cards deal 27 cards *face-up* in three piles of 9. Ask someone to remember any card as you deal them. You now ask which pile it is in. Pick up the cards so that the pile containing the chosen card is in the middle. Turn the cards over.

Deal the cards out, turning each one face-up as you do so. Ask which pile the chosen card is in. Again pick up the piles so that the one containing the chosen card is in the middle.

Turn the cards over and deal them out face-up as before. Ask which pile the chosen card is in. You then announce the name of the chosen card.

Method: the chosen card will always be the middle one in the stated pile.

Explanation of the trick requires careful thought. There is an interesting connection with base three numbers.

Variations include bringing the chosen card to any stated position by picking up the piles in certain orders, and stating the position of the chosen card having allowed the spectator to pick up the piles in any order.

4 Geometrical tricks

A square measuring 8 cm by 8 cm is made of four pieces of card. The area is 64 cm². They are arranged as shown and they then form a rectangle measuring 5 cm by 13 cm – with area 65 cm²!

Explain.

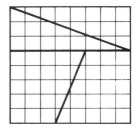

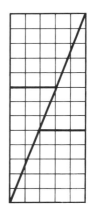

There is an interesting connection with the Fibonacci sequence: 5, 8, 13 are three consecutive terms of the Fibonacci sequence. Any three consecutive terms can be used to form the square and rectangle.

References

M. Gardner, *Mathematics, Magic and Mystery* (Dover), *Mathematical Puzzles and Diversions*, *More Mathematical Puzzles and Diversions*, *Further Mathematical Diversions*, *Mathematical Carnival*, and *Mathematical Circus* (Penguin)

25 ▪ Monopoly

Most people have played and enjoyed Monopoly at some time. It inevitably involves handling money but it is also open to some interesting mathematical analysis which can lead to more sophisticated playing strategies.

1 The probabilities of landing on different properties from a given starting point depend on the likely occurrence of the totals 2, 3, . . . 12 when throwing two dice, and these vary considerably. These can be determined and applied to the game. What for example is the probability of paying either Super Tax or Income Tax (or both!) when leaving Liverpool Street Station?

When it is your turn calculate the probability of landing on your opponents' properties and use this as a guide to how much money you can invest in putting up houses as against having cash in hand to pay rent.

2 Analyse the Chance and Community Chest cards to see whether you think they are biased for or against you. Would the situation be different at different stages in the game?

3 Compare the likely returns on the same outlay on different properties. Is it better to spend £400 on Mayfair or £400 on two stations? Compare the costs of putting up a hotel on the Old Kent Road with one on Pentonville Road. Which gives the better return on the investment?

4 Is it better to pay to come out of jail or to take a chance on a double?

5 What is the probability that you move from Go to Free Parking using only Chance, Community Chest or Visiting Jail spaces?

References

A Monopoly game
B. Bolt, *Even More Mathematical Activities*, activity 120 (Cambridge University Press)

26 ▪ Snooker

Snooker originated in Jubbulpore, India, in 1875 and has steadily gained in popularity so that it is now watched by millions on television. The ability to pot a ball accurately, to play a ball off the cushioned walls and to pace the cue ball to leave it just right for the next shot is the essence of the game. How can this be achieved?

1

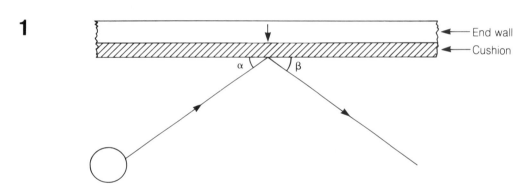

Mark a point near the middle of one end wall of a snooker table. Hit the cue ball to strike this point at an angle α and note the angle β at which it rebounds. Repeat this for a wide range of angles (try to avoid putting spin on the cue ball). Plot a graph of β against α. If the table is in a good condition then the graph should approximate to the line β = α, showing that the ball bounces off the cushion as if it were a light ray being reflected off a mirror.

What would you find if the cushion became hard? Experiment by placing a piece of wood against the cushion and seeing how the ball rebounds off it.

How would spin affect your findings?

Experiment to see if it is possible to make the angle β larger than α.

2 Because the balls are *reflected* off the cushions, players can use this knowledge to strike cue balls in such a way that they bounce off one or more cushions before making contact with a coloured target ball when they have been snookered (i.e. placed in a position by their opponent that the ball they must hit is hidden behind other balls they must avoid).

Investigate ways of using mirror images to determine how the cue ball must be hit. See activity 91 in Bolt, *Mathematical Activities*, for a detailed discussion of this.

3

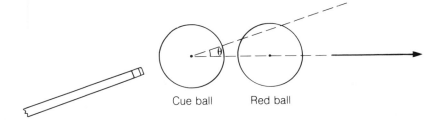

Cue ball   Red ball

(a) When a cue ball hits a coloured ball at an angle the coloured ball will move off at an angle θ to the direction at which the cue ball was travelling before impact. Draw the above diagram to see how this is achieved. What is the largest angle θ which can be produced in practice? If the cue ball is standing on the black spot and a red ball is placed along the centre line of the table, how far towards the D can it be placed to be still pottable in a centre pocket?

(b) By experimenting, find the angle between the directions of the cue ball and a coloured ball after impact. If the balls were perfectly elastic it would be 90°. What happens to the balls if they are in line?

4 How accurately must a ball be struck to enter a pocket? The black ball is a frequent target for potting when it is on its spot at the head of the table. Find the range of angles through which it can be hit to enter a top pocket.

5 The amount a ball slows down (a) while rolling, (b) through hitting a cushion, are important factors which a player must take into account when hitting a ball. Design experiments to investigate the retardation.

6 How is spin important to a cue ball? What is its effect and how is it used? At approximately what height should a cue strike a cue ball so that it rolls across the table without spinning?

7 Suppose that at the point when all the red balls are potted, that all of the coloured balls are on their spots. Show a sequence of shots and the path of the cue ball for a player to pot all the coloured balls.

8 Show examples of how a player sets up a snooker giving the positions of all the relevant balls before and after the shot.

9 See what you can find out about the properties of the elliptical pool tables which were sold in the USA in the mid-sixties.

References

B. Bolt, *Mathematical Activities* (Cambridge University Press)

L. Mottershead, *Sources of Mathematical Discovery* (Blackwell)

C. B. Daish, *The Physics of Ball Games* (English Universities Press)

The Sigma Project, *Billiards*

The Spode Group, *GCSE Coursework Assignments* (Hodder and Stoughton)

27 ▪ Gambling

Gambling is a popular activity
– horse racing, football pools,
fruit machines, Premium
Bonds – and many young
people will have knowledge of
it through their parents. A
study of the mathematics of
gambling might convince
some pupils that the chances
of winning are usually very
remote.

1 Horse racing

3.55 JOHN BECKETT MAIDEN STAKES (£828: 1m 6f) (5)

5	**00 GUESSING (BF)** (K Abdulla) G Harwood 3–8–7 . . . . **A Clark 2**
7	**0 MOWSOOM (USA)** (Sheikh Mohammed) H Cecil 3–8–7 . . . . **N Day 1**
11	**02 TAMATOUR (USA)** (H H Aga Khan) M Stoute 3–8–7 . . . . **A Kimberley 3**
16	**0024 PARSON'S CHILD (USA)(BF)** (R Stokes) I Cumani 3–8–4 . . . . . . **P Hamblett 5**
17	**0003 TONQUIN** (A Morrison) J Toller 3–8–4 . . . . **G Duffield 4**

11–10 Tamatour, 3–1 Guessing, 11–2 Mowsoom, Parsons Child, 10–1 Tonquin.

If you put £1 on each horse and Tamatour won
would you make a profit? And if Tonquin
won? By putting different amounts on each
horse, is it possible to guarantee that you will
make a profit?

The racing page of a newspaper is a useful
source of data for this theme of beating the
bookmaker. See Bolt, *EMMA*, activity 115.

2 Roulette wheels

The Monte Carlo version of the roulette
wheel has 37 sections, marked 0 to 36. You bet
on any number and, if you win, you get 35
times the amount you staked and also your
stake is returned. If you staked £1 on each
section you would pay out £37 and receive
£36: this is a long-run loss of about 2.7%.
Apart from the 0, half of the sections are red
and half are black. Suppose you stake £1 on
red. If it comes up, you win £1 and your stake
is returned. You lose on the black and get 50p
on the 0. A simple calculation shows that the
bank wins at a rate of about 1.35%.

Play the game (but not for money!) to test
the theory.

Small plastic roulette wheels are available
at toy shops. Alternatively, a home-made
spinner can be designed.

The layout of the casino table and further
details of the game are given in Arnold, *The
Complete Book of Indoor Games*.

3 Gambling systems

Various systems for winning when gambling have been proposed. One is the *martingale*. It is usually applied to games where the probability of winning is 0.5 each time – for example, coin tossing. You bet £1, say, initially. If you win you get £1 and also your stake money is returned. You continue to bet £1 every time you win. But when you lose, you double your bet the next time. So, if you finish following a win, you will make a profit. Is there a snag? Try the system with coin tossing or betting on colours on a roulette wheel.

Another system is the *anti-martingale*. You decide how many successive wins you are prepared to accept. Suppose you choose 5. You double your stake each time, giving up as soon as you lose once, or when you have won 5 times straight off. If you lose, you only lose £1, if you win, you gain £31. Is there a snag?

4 Premium Bonds

Find out how ERNIE works and the distribution of prizes.

5 Fruit machines

Analyse the workings of a fruit machine.

6 Football pools

Devise a system to predict football results based on the previous three or four weeks' results. Compare it with a method based on random numbers.

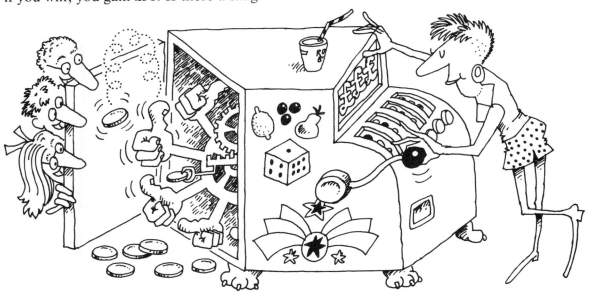

References

D. Huff, *How to Take a Chance* (Penguin)

P. Arnold (ed.), *The Complete Book of Indoor Games* (Hamlyn)

P. Arnold, *The Encyclopedia of Gambling* (Collins)

B. Bolt, *Even More Mathematical Activities (EMMA)* (Cambridge University Press)

28 ▪ Simulating games on a computer

Games have a strong motivation for many children. Some suggestions are given here for simulating games by computer. There are opportunities for keen programmers to go further and demonstrate their skills with graphics.

1 Craps

In the game of craps two dice are thrown. If the total is 7 or 11, the player wins immediately. If the total is 2, 3 or 12 the player loses immediately. If any other total is thrown (that is, 4, 5, 6, 8, 9, 10) the player continues to throw the dice until they either get that same total again, in which case they win, or they get a 7, in which case they lose.

The game can be simulated by computer using statements of the form
A = RND(6) : B = RND(6) : X = A + B
IF X = 7 OR X = 11 THEN PRINT "Win"
etc.

The relative frequency in a large number of games can be found.

A theoretical analysis (within the capabilities of able 15 or 16 year olds) shows that the probability of winning is $\frac{244}{495}$ and a player can expect to lose about 1.4% of the stakes in the long run.

2 Beetle

In the game of Beetle the parts of a beetle are drawn when certain numbers are thrown with a die.

First, a six has to be thrown in order to draw the body.

Then, in any order,
a five for the head
a four for the tail
4 threes for the legs.

When the five has been thrown, the eyes can be drawn – 2 ones required – and the feelers – 2 twos – again, in any order.

The winner is the first person to complete a beetle.

By simulating the game the average number of throws needed can be found. A computer program could include the appropriate graphics to draw the beetle.

3 Snakes and ladders

In the game of snakes and ladders a die is thrown and a counter moved appropriately on a board. When the counter is on the foot of a ladder it moves up to the top of the ladder; when it is on the mouth of a snake, it moves down the snake. The winner is the first person to get to the final square. Usually a six has to be thrown to start the game.

The length of the game depends on the number and positions of the snakes and the ladders. The games on some boards can go on for too long and the players become tired. The idea is to design a board which will finish in a reasonable number of throws on average.

One method to simulate the game is to number the squares from 1 to 100 imagining them in a long line (see the diagram below).

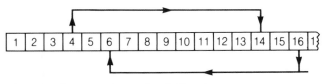 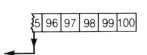

Then instructions such as the following can be used:

X = RND(6) : P = P + X
IF P = 4 THEN P = 14
IF P = 16 THEN P = 6
etc.

The position after each throw could be printed. Expert computer programmers might like to display the board and the positions on the screen.

References

P. Arnold, *The Encyclopedia of Gambling* (Collins)

P. Arnold, *The Complete Book of Indoor Games* (Hamlyn)

F. R. Watson, *An Introduction to Simulation* (University of Keele)

29 ▪ Planning a new kitchen

In larger towns, centres exist just for selling fitted kitchens, many DIY centres and furniture shops stock a wide range of kitchen units while a Yellow Pages telephone directory contains pages of kitchen planners. Because of all the kits available for putting together kitchen units the DIY enthusiast is well able to produce a fitted kitchen at a fraction of the cost it would take to employ a professional, but it will only be a success if it is carefully planned, researched and costed. Here the various activities are best done in order, starting with a collection of brochures.

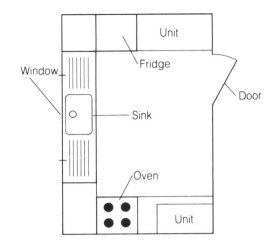

1 Visit local centres which sell kitchen units and collect a range of brochures giving the kinds of units available with their sizes and costs.

2 Make a floor plan and wall plans of the room which is to be fitted out as a kitchen. Measure carefully and draw the plans on squared paper to a convenient scale. Note the positions of doors, windows, and electricity points and switches. The latter may need to be moved.

3 Decide what kind of sink unit and oven to have and where they are to go on the plan. Will space be needed for a refrigerator, washing machine, central heating unit? If so, position them to best advantage. Plan the standing units to avoid gaps and decide how to have the working surface.

4 Decide on the wall units and where they will be fixed so that they are not in the way but can be reached.

5 Where would you suggest electricity power points to be placed and what lighting would you recommend?

6 Will any tiling be necessary?

7 What kind of floor covering would you recommend?

8 Write a report for the imaginary householder with your recommendations for the kitchen giving reasons for your choice of units and design of the layout and details of the costs involved. Alternatives and options could be part of the scheme.

9 Make a model of the kitchen.

References

Brochures available in DIY centres, etc.

30 ▪ Decorating and furnishing a room

Many teenagers are interested in planning their own bedroom, or opportunities might arise for them to help their parents in planning some other room. Information about paint, wallpaper, furniture and carpets is readily available in many shops.

1 Decorating a room

A simple project would be to plan the decoration of the room – painting and wallpapering.

Choose colours for the paint and select the wallpaper, bearing in mind permanent features of the room such as the floor covering and the furniture. Many books on decorating give advice about colour matching.

Estimate (a) the amount of paint needed (the approximate coverage is usually stated on the tin), and (b) the number of rolls of wallpaper (tables are available in shops giving the number of rolls needed, although it is interesting to estimate it yourself. Wallpapering involves a linear measurement problem rather than area. Allowance needs to be made for matching the pattern.)

Estimate the cost. If this is more than can be afforded decide how the cost can be reduced.

2 Furnishing a room

A more involved project might be to plan the furnishing of the room. For this purpose a scale drawing of the room on squared paper would be useful. Pieces of card can be cut to represent furniture and moved around to obtain suitable circulation space. Books on design often contain recommendations about space needed.

In planning the carpet consideration needs to be given to widths available; also pieces removed for a cupboard, say, might be usable elsewhere.

The position of light fittings and power points could also be planned.

References

Leaflets about paint, carpets, etc. are available in shops.

N. Nieswand, *The Complete Interior Designer* (Macdonald Orbis)

J. Blake, *How to Solve Your Interior Design Problems* (Hamlyn)

31 ▪ Ideal home

Designing a flat, bungalow or house is always a good starting point for a project which can develop in many ways. The activities here build up to doing a design specification for a house.

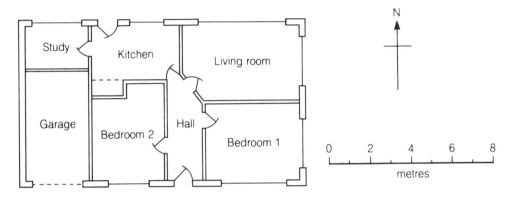

1 Preliminary research is important before trying to draw a *plan* of your ideal home. It is helpful to look at a variety of houses or house details to get an idea of the appropriate types of rooms and their sizes and the ways in which they are interconnected.

(a) Visit the homes of friends and relatives and make sketches of their floor plans, trying to see the advantages and drawbacks.

(b) House agents will often be helpful in giving away spare copies of the details of houses which they have had for sale.

(c) Try to find an architect's drawing of a house.

2 Make a list of the rooms you want to include in your design. It may help to make cut-outs of the floor plans of the rooms you want to include to a suitable scale and then investigate ways in which they might fit together like a jigsaw. Try to imagine living in the space you are creating and see how conveniently rooms are connected. Do you

want built-in cupboards/wardrobes? Avoid too many doors in a room. The plan shown above looks fine initially, but there is no provision for a bathroom or toilet so it would never get planning permission. It is also poor planning to build a house where the main living area faces away from the sun. Now make a detailed plan of your ideal home.

3 Before drawing the *elevations* go for a walk around your locality and make a note of the houses you like the look of with sketches of the shape and style of windows, doors, roofs. Draw as many elevations as you think necessary to make your design clear.

4 Make an isometric or perspective drawing of your design.

References

House agents, magazines about the home, books on geometric drawing
SMP, *New Book 5* (Cambridge University Press)

32 ▪ Moving house

Moving house is a common experience for many people. This project explores several aspects of a move, including compiling a house agent's handout, calculating heating costs and rates, professional fees, removal expenses, furnishings, and borrowing money.

1 House agent's services

(a) Imagine your house is for sale. How would house agents describe it in their typical advertising literature? Visit a house agent and obtain some handouts of houses for sale and use them as a basis to compile one of your own house.

(b) What are the costs involved in selling your house through a house agent? What are the advantages and disadvantages of having your house on the books of more than one agent?

2 Running costs

Obtain the details of a house of the kind you would like to move to. Be realistic! Is it likely to cost more or less to live in? Compare the rateable value and method of heating.

3 Professional's fees

How much will it cost to have the house surveyed?

How much will you have to pay the solicitor for

(a) selling your house,

(b) buying a different house?

4 Moving costs

Moving your furniture costs money. Try to obtain estimates from local removal firms of the cost of removal and compare this with the cost of hiring a self-drive lorry/van. Remember that the self-drive lorry will probably require several journeys so that if the house move is a long way it will need to be hired for several days.

5 Furnishing costs

Assume that the new house will require floor coverings and curtains. Investigate the costs of different floor coverings and curtain materials and estimate the total cost entailed.

6 Money management

It is likely that a house move will entail borrowing money. Investigate the costs of borrowing £30,000 from banks and building societies.

References

House agents, removal companies, banks, building societies, solicitors

D. Lewis, *Teach Yourself: Buying, Selling and Moving Home* (Hodder and Stoughton)

33 ▪ DIY secondary double-glazing

There is much emphasis these days on energy conservation, and one way to reduce significantly the heat loss from a house is to double-glaze the windows. DIY centres stock a wide range of materials for doing this and the planning and costing of such an operation for a number of windows in a known house would form the basis of a worthwhile project.

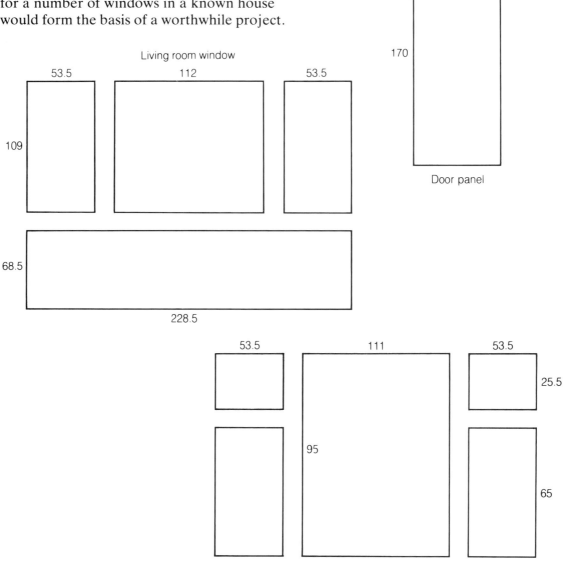

Background to a practical project

(a) The diagrams opposite represent the real problem faced by one of the authors in 1986. The windows and door panel were carefully measured to the nearest half centimetre, although experience has shown that many builders' materials are often measured in imperial units. The measurements were double checked before drawing scale diagrams.

(b) Visits to the two largest DIY stores in the locality indicated a large range of possibilities. The first job was to make very rough estimates of the costs of using the various schemes before deciding on detailed estimates of the ones in the range which could be afforded.

(c) Details of the most likely schemes were then taken home for closer analysis. The final scheme decided upon was based on the use of acrylic sheets and plastic edging strips, and the materials were only sold in the following sizes:

Acrylic sheets
1.83 m × 0.61 m   £7
1.22 m × 0.61 m   £5
1.22 m × 1.22 m   £9.60
1.22 m × 1.83 m   £14.60

Plastic edging packs
2 lengths of 1.22 m   £2.99
2 lengths of 1.83 m   £3.99
2 lengths of 1.22 m, one hinged   £3.29
2 lengths of 1.83 m, one hinged   £4.29

Pack of 10 turn catches with screws   £2.49

1 (a) Work out the materials needed to be purchased to double-glaze the above windows. How would you cut up the sheets you buy in the most efficient way? Note the window measurements given are to the edge of the glass and the acrylic will need to overlap the frames by about 1.5 cm. What does your solution cost?

(b) The bottom pane in the living room caused a problem. How would you solve it? In addition to the above materials it was necessary to purchase a special glue to stick the edging to the acrylic, and a special tool to cut the acrylic.

(c) Visit a local DIY store and work out the cost for an alternative scheme at current prices.

2 Estimate the cost of double-glazing a room in your own house.

References

Brochures from DIY centres, etc.

34 ▪ Loft conversions

House owners often consider extending their accommodation by building a room in the roof. Making a survey of a roof space and planning how it may be converted is a valuable exercise in surveying and scale drawing which requires spatial insight and the ability to interpret building regulations.

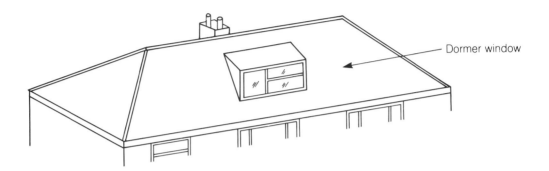

Dormer window

1 Make a careful survey of a roof space to which you have access, and draw its plan and elevations.

2 Any height of less than 107 cm (3 ft 6 in) is only really good for storage so use this fact to determine the limit of the usable floor area.

3 Building regulations demand that at least half the area which has a headroom of 150 cm (5 ft) or more must in fact have a minimum headroom of 230 cm (7 ft 7 in).

See if a dormer window could be fitted to fulfil these conditions and achieve a worthwhile space.

4 For a room to be habitable (i.e. not just a box room) the regulations require that the total area of ventilation must be not less than one-twentieth of the floor area, and the window area must not be less than one-tenth of the floor area.

Make sure your design fulfils these criteria.

5 Access to your space is essential. You will need a plan of the floor below the roof to see where a staircase or loft ladder can be fitted. Investigate the design of loft ladders.

6 If your proposed room adds less than 50 m^3 (1765 ft^3) or 10% of the original house, up to a maximum of 115 m^3 (4061 ft^3), planning permission is not required as long as new building does not go above the ridge of the roof or beyond the outside walls. Check whether or not your proposal requires planning permission.

References

Various books have been written on the subject such as:

J. W. W. Eykyn, *All You Need to Know about Loft Conversions* (Collins)

35 ▪ In the garden

In many households interest is shown in various aspects of gardening, and this is sometimes shared by the children. A project on gardening could provide an opportunity for parental involvement.

1 Growing your own vegetables

The intention of this project is to find the cost of growing your own vegetables, possibly aiming to be self-supporting throughout the year.

Devise a planting plan for your own garden at home or for a standard allotment measuring 30 feet by 90 feet (approximately 9 metres by 30 metres).

Some points to consider:
- the cost of seeds and plants
- the cost of fertilisers, weed-killers, etc.
- the cost of tools
- the cost of your labour (or is gardening a hobby?)
- the quantity consumed of each type of vegetable
- the amount of space needed by each type of vegetable
- a rotation system
- the cost of storage (e.g. deep-freeze).

2 The use of fertilisers

The intention is to investigate the effect of fertilisers by carrying out an experiment in growing marrows, say. Apply various treatments to the marrow plants. Some plants could be used as a control group and not be given any special treatment. Ensure that the soil condition is the same for all the plants. Keep a regular record of the lengths of the marrows and at the end of the experiment weigh them. Write up a report which would be suitable for a gardening magazine.

3 Yield

Compare the yields of different varieties of peas, beans, potatoes or tomatoes.

4 Lawns

How much does it cost to maintain a lawn? Some points to consider:

- the cost of a lawnmower (how many years is it expected to last?)
- the cost of electricity or petrol and oil
- the cost of servicing
- the cost of any other tools used (for example, spikers, rakers)
- the cost of fertilisers and weed-killers
- the time taken to mow the lawn (does it depend on the length of the grass?)

What is the most efficient way to cut the lawn? (See the diagrams on the right.)

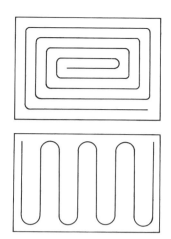

5 Up the garden path

Design a garden path or patio using paving slabs. Slabs are available in a variety of shapes and colours. Work out the cost of your plans.

6 Designing a garden

Plan a garden for a new house – lawns, borders, rockery, shrubs, fruit trees, etc.

References

Gardening catalogues are a useful source of information. Visit a garden centre.

R. Genders, *The Allotment Garden* (John Gifford)

I. G. Walls, *Growing Vegetables, Fruit and Flowers for Profit* (David and Charles)

J. Bond (ed.), *The Good Food Growing Guide* (David and Charles)

36 ▪ Where has all the electricity gone?

Every quarter most households are faced with an electricity bill. The head of the household may well have an inquisition and demand that the family uses less electricity next quarter. Most people are not very aware of the relative costs of using different pieces of equipment, for all they have to do is press a switch in each case. This project starts by looking at the power consumption of all the different pieces of electrical equipment in a house and ends by making recommendations on how bills could be reduced.

What is a *unit* of electrical energy? This is the energy used by a piece of apparatus such as a one bar fire rated at 1 kW (1000 watts) used for one hour, or by a 100 watt bulb burning for ten hours. It is this which is measured by the electricity meter and on which the electricity board works out its bill. In 1986, for example, a typical semi-detached house used 1466 units in the second quarter and was charged at 5.49p a unit giving £80.48, on top of which there was a standing quarterly charge of £7.80 giving a total bill of £88.28.

1 Make a list of all the electrical equipment in your house with the power rating of each piece: every light bulb, kettle, toaster, oven, television, record player, fire, storage heater, immersion heater, hair dryer, shower, food mixer, iron, washing machine, refrigerator, deep-freeze, vacuum cleaner, electric drill, etc.

2 Estimate the time for which each piece of equipment is used. It is perhaps more important to measure for how long a 3 kW

kettle is used than a 60 watt bulb, but a large number of lights are used for long periods and so cannot be ignored. The tricky ones to estimate will be those operated by a thermostat such as immersion heaters and refrigerators. How will your estimate differ for different parts of the year?

3 Take the latest electricity bill for your house and try to show where all the units for which your house has been charged have been used. Illustrate your findings with a pie chart or pictogram.

4 Recommend ways in which your household could reduce bills such as: using showers instead of baths; using night storage heaters on a lower tariff; only putting enough water in the kettle for immediate needs; not using a running hot tap to wash dishes; using fluorescent lights instead of bulbs.

References

Electricity bills, leaflets from local electricity board

37 ▪ Energy conservation

As fossil-fuels begin to run out, considerable publicity is given to methods of saving energy in the home. A project on this topic could involve parental interest and might result in financial savings.

First assess where the money goes.

STEP ONE: ADDING IT UP
add up all your bills for gas and electricity for a year if you keep them. Add to them what you spend on oil or paraffin heating, coal and wood. Fuel bill fact: up to about 80p in the £ of your fuel bills can go on heating your home and providing hot water.

If you want to find out where the money goes in your house, move to:

STEP TWO: TRACKING IT DOWN
for two, three or four weeks do three things.

● Read your gas and electricity meters *at the same time every day.* (You can get leaflets on how to do it from your fuel board offices.) Then write the readings down. Work out how many hods or buckets of coal, how much oil or paraffin you've used and write this down too each day.

● Keep a *diary* at the end of each day on the main things you think may have altered your energy use that day. Did you heat the house longer or shorter? Was the weather warmer or colder? Did you heat more or fewer rooms? Did you have more or fewer baths? Did you use more or less water? What appliances did you use?

● Make graphs of the daily figures of energy use, and try to work out how the daily changes might be caused by the different things noted in the diary. If they don't seem to make sense, go on for a bit longer and look for other causes. Did anyone come to stay? Have other members of the family been using appliances, opening doors and windows to let heat out, turning up radiators, doing extra cooking?

Another method is to record your energy consumption for hot water and for other uses (television, lighting, etc) in the summer, when the space heating is off. Do the same again during the winter months and simple subtraction will give a reasonable guide to the amount of energy you are using to heat the house.

STEP THREE: REACHING A JUDGEMENT.
Decide: is your home like the one in the fuel bill fact above? Or is there something special about it? Do you really need to use all the energy you do use? Or might you be comfortable for less money – for instance if your home were better insulated – now you have some idea of where the money goes? Now read the rest of this book, and see what it's best to do.

1 What does it cost to heat your house? A useful procedure is given in the booklet *Make the Most of Your Heating*, published by the Energy Efficiency Office. Carry out the steps recommended.

2 The diagram at the top of this page is taken from a British Gas advertisement. Further information about heat loss is in the Energy Efficiency Office's booklet, and methods of reducing it are explained. Find out the costs of various methods of insulation and estimate how much they are likely to save.

3 Heating engineers refer to U values. Find out about them and use them to calculate the heat loss in your house. (Johnson, *Beginner's Guide to Central Heating*, includes a heat loss sheet showing how to work out the heat loss for each room of a house.)

References

The booklets *Make the Most of Your Heating* and *Cutting Home Energy Costs* are available free from the Energy Efficiency Office, Room 1312, Thames House South, Millbank, London SW1P 4QJ

W. H. Johnson, *Beginner's Guide to Central Heating* (Newnes)

SMP, *New Book 5* (Cambridge University Press)

38 ▪ The cost of keeping a pet

Many pupils have a cat or a dog at home. Others might have smaller animals such as guinea pigs, gerbils, rabbits, etc. Some might even have a pony or at least be interested in finding how much it would cost.

1 The cost of a domestic pet

The following points could be considered:
(a) What was the original cost of obtaining the animal?
(b) Allow for occasional expenses:
 ● Equipment. For example, basket, lead, collar, brushes, dishes, etc. An estimate of the number of these items needed during the animal's life will be needed.
 ● Cost of having the animal looked after when you are away.
 ● Vet's costs.
(c) Estimate the regular expenses:
 ● The cost of food: fresh, tinned, dried.
 ● Medication: coat conditioners, vitamins, etc.
(d) Can you make a profit from breeding?
 The cost during the estimated lifetime can be found, and also the weekly or daily cost.
 The costs of different breeds of dogs could be compared or the cost of a cat could be compared with that of a dog.

2 The cost of a pony

Some points to consider:
(a) The cost of obtaining the pony.
(b) Occasional expenses:
 ● Equipment.
 ● Vet's costs.
(c) Regular expenses: food, etc.
(d) Cost of accommodation.
(e) Rental of field.
(f) Riding equipment and clothes.

References

P. Donald, *The Pony Trap* (Weidenfeld and Nicholson)
The Reader's Digest, *Illustrated Book of Dogs*

39 ▪ The cost of a wedding

Some pupils might have older brothers or sisters who are getting married and the cost of the wedding might well have been a talking-point at home. Others might like to look ahead to their own wedding. The size of th[e] expense usually comes as a shock.

1 Some possible items to consider are:

(a) Clothes
 • The cost of the bride's dress and accoutrements (shoes, etc.). Are they being bought or made at home?
 • The cost of the bridegroom's clothes. Bought or hired?
 • The cost of the bridesmaids' clothes. Who pays?

(b) The ceremony
 • At a church. The cost of the service. Choir? Bellringers?
 • At a registry office. Standard fee.
 • The cost of flowers.

(c) The cost of the wedding ring(s)

(d) Transport
 • The cost of the wedding car and cars for guests.
 • The cost of travel if the wedding is taking place in another part of the country.

(e) The reception
 • The cost of the cake.
 • The cost of food and drink: buffet or sit-down; in a restaurant or in a hall or at home; the number of guests.

(f) The cost of photographs

(g) The cost of the honeymoon

(h) Some of the expenses might be offset by the value of the presents the couple might expect to receive.

The items could be classified according to who is paying for them. What is the major item of cost? Where could economies be made if necessary?

2 Write an article for a magazine or newspaper about the cost of a wedding. Devise a fill-in sheet which would enable readers to estimate the cost of a wedding.

References

P. & W. Derraugh, *Wedding Etiquette* (Foulsham)

40 · The real cost of sport

Many people take part in sport both at school and when they are older, and an increasing amount of money is spent by people on leisure activities. There is plenty of potential in this area to consider what it costs to play a particular sport and/or what individuals spend on the sports they play or watch.

1 Your own costs

Investigate what you, or your parents, spend on your sporting activities in a typical year.
(a) What sports do you participate in (i) at school, (ii) out of school?
(b) What equipment did you need to buy for your sports such as rackets, bats, balls, boots, shoes, track suit, sports clothing and what did they cost?
(c) How often do you need to replace equipment, for example, a shuttle cock or squash ball? How long does a racket last before it needs to be restrung or replaced?
(d) What does it cost you to play sports out of school, in club membership, court fees, transport etc.?
(e) If you play for a team, what does it cost to play in matches?
(f) How much do you spend as a spectator of sport?
(g) Do you spend money on books or magazines on sport?
(h) Do you spend money on being coached?

2 The comparative costs of different sports

There is a wide variation in the requirements for different sports. Some require the purchase of expensive equipment such as a canoe, or sail board, or golf clubs, while others may require a substantial court fee every time you play as for tennis or squash. If you play for a team outside of school then you will normally be expected to pay a match fee to contribute to the cost of travel, hire of a pitch, and entertaining the opposing team. Equipment wears out and needs replacing or repair, this also needs to be considered.

Choose two or three sports from those familiar to you and compare the annual costs of each for a typical participant. It would be interesting to choose sports which are as different as possible such as fishing, snooker and hockey.

References

Sports equipment shops and sports clubs, local libraries and information centres

41 · Buying or renting a TV

Buying a television can involve spending several hundred pounds. Also, when a television goes wrong it can be expensive to put right. Some people prefer to rent a television rather than buy one because it does not require a large initial outlay and the rental company will replace it or repair it if there is a fault. A comparison of the costs of buying and renting can form the basis of a project.

1 Buying a TV

The following points need to be considered when buying a television.

(a) What type of television is required? Screen size, portable, colour, Teletext facilities, etc.
(b) What is the cost of buying such a television? Visit shops to compare prices and find out about special offers. Obtain the cost of hire purchase also.
(c) Estimate the cost of repairs. This might require a survey asking people who own their televisions how much they have spent on repairs.
(d) Find the cost of yearly insurance (the first year is usually guaranteed). Compare with the estimated cost of repairs.
(e) How will the value of the television depreciate? What would its second-hand value be after 1 year, 2 years, etc.?

2 Renting a TV

Obtain information about the cost of renting the same model.

3 Comparing the cost

The two methods can be compared by finding costs year by year (the costs of the licence and the electricity are the same for both methods). Is there a stage when the buying method becomes cheaper? How are the costs influenced by changes in insurance, rental, etc.?

Write up your findings as a *Which?*-style report.

References

TV rental shops – consult *Yellow Pages* telephone directory

42 • A holiday abroad

Many pupils will have a holiday abroad with their family or with a school group and may have sufficient experience to be able to plan a holiday for themselves. A project on this theme provides an opportunity for budgeting in an interesting and unfamiliar context. It could be written up as if for a magazine article or for a television programme on holidays.

First, decide where you want to go, for how long, at what time of year, and how much money you have available.

1 Study newspaper advertisements, visit travel agents, read guidebooks, obtain maps. Are you going on a package tour or are you planning the details yourself?

2 The major items of cost will be:
(a) Accommodation: full-board hotel, semi-board hotel, rented accommodation, camping, youth hostelling, etc.
(b) Food: cost of eating out, cost of preparing own food.
(c) Travel: getting there – boat, rail, coach, plane, car. Student concessions.
(d) What to do when you are there: activities, sightseeing, transport.

3 Preliminary planning will be needed for:
(a) Passport
(b) Insurance (including medical)
(c) Clothes
(d) Arrangements for money: obtaining currency and traveller's cheques, exchange rates, commission costs.

References

Brochures from travel agents, guidebooks
F. Powell, *A Consumer's Guide to Holidays Abroad* (Telegraph Publications)

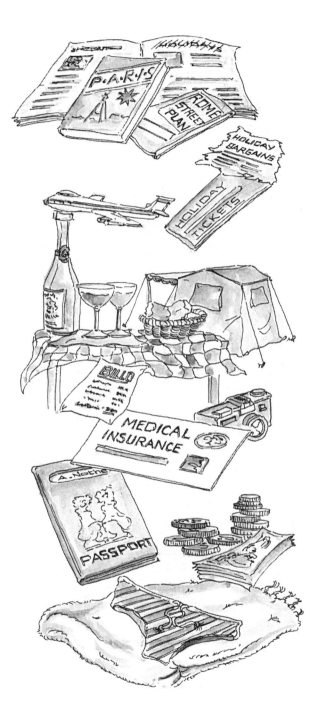

43 . The cost of running ballet/driving/ riding schools

What is a fair price for driving lessons? Why should pony riding be so expensive? How can you make a living from running a ballet school? Trying to answer questions such as these gives insight into the economics of running a small business.

1 Running a ballet school

Consider the economics of a small ballet school:
(a) What accommodation is used? If hired what does it cost? Who pays for cleaning? Heating is important and costs. Rates?
(b) How many classes are run in a typical week and how big are the classes? What is the largest number of classes a teacher could reasonably take in a week, remembering that most of them will be in the early evening and Saturdays?
(c) Is a pianist used or a record-player? What are the related costs?
(d) If the owner employs teachers, what does this cost?
(e) What does advertising cost?
(f) Is special insurance required?

Use what you can find out to show how a person can make a reasonable living by running a ballet school and what should be charged for the lessons.

2 Running a driving school

Try to determine a fair price for a driving lesson by considering the facts:

(a) The cost of buying, maintaining, and running a car is high.
(b) Lessons can only be given to one pupil at a time and the instructor has to be paid.
(c) Insurance cover is expensive and lessons cannot take place when cars are off the road for repairs.
(d) A car depreciates in value and has a limited useful life.

3 Running a riding stable

(a) What is the cost of a pony/horse?
(b) What is the useful working life of a pony and for how many hours a day can it be used?
(c) Food is a very significant factor for ponies have to be fed whether they are used or not.
(d) What are the farrier costs and vet's bills?
(e) What special equipment such as saddles are needed?

Having considered all the running costs for such an establishment try to decide the minimum number of ponies and the hire charges and lesson charges the owner would have to make in order to make a reasonable living.

44 ▪ The cost of running a farm

This topic might appeal to some pupils from a rural background. Many simplifying assumptions will need to be made, possibly restricting the project initially to either a livestock or an arable farm.

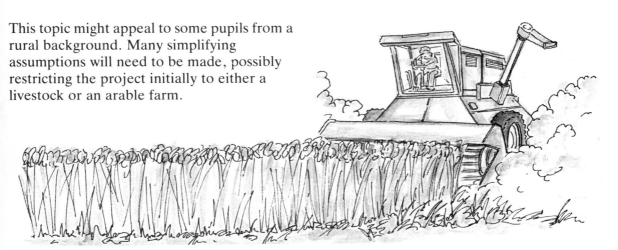

1 Livestock

First, decide what the farm will be like. What type of livestock will be farmed? How much land will be required (sheep and cattle need a large amount)? What accommodation, equipment and machinery will be needed? (Dairy cattle, for example, need milking equipment.)

Secondly, consider the cost. What will the initial cost of the animals be? How much will the land cost to buy (probably prohibitive) or to rent? What will be the cost of buildings, equipment, machinery, food, labour? Will you need to borrow money to set up the farm? How much interest will have to be paid on this money? Is there a government subsidy or grant available?

Thirdly, estimate the profit. How much will the animals sell for? Consider the income and expenditure year by year. How long will the farm take to be profitable? What is the most significant item of expenditure? How sensitive is profit to changes in costs? Does a larger number of animals produce an increased profit? How can the profit be maximised?

2 Arable

First, decide what crops you will grow, how much land will be required, what machinery and storage accommodation will be needed.

Secondly, estimate the cost: seeds, machinery, labour, rent, fertilisers, weed-killers, etc.

Thirdly, work out the profit. Estimate the yield and how much the crops will sell for. Consider the income and expenditure year by year. How long will the farm take to be profitable? What is the most significant item of expenditure? How sensitive is profit to changes in costs? Does planting a larger amount of land produce an increase in profits? How can the profit be maximised?

3 Mixed farming

A comparison of the costs of a livestock farm and an arable farm could be made and a combination of the two considered.

References

Farming journals, manufacturers' catalogues
The Spode Group, *Solving Real Problems with Mathematics, Vol. 2* (Cranfield Press)

45 ▪ Financial arithmetic

Newspaper advertisements for building societies, banks, etc. are now commonplace. Many pupils have their own savings account and are interested in financial matters. This is a topic in which an approach through projects can achieve more than formal lessons through 'sums'.

1 Investing money

Obtain information about investment in building societies, National Savings Certificates, National Savings Investment account, banks, etc.

How is interest calculated? What do 'gross' and 'net' mean?

What does 'compounded half yearly' mean? Do you have to pay tax?

Advise someone on how to invest (a) £100, (b) £5000.

How long would it take to double your money?

A short computer program could be written to show the growth of money with compound interest.

2 Borrowing money

What does it cost to borrow money from a bank or a financial company?

How does hire purchase work? Compare the cost of buying a car or motorbike outright with the cost of buying it through hire purchase.

Find out about credit cards – generally usable cards such as Access, Barclaycard, etc. and cards usable only in particular shops. What does it cost to borrow money in this way? Compare the cost with that of loans from banks, etc. How much credit can you get from shops in the High Street?

Find out about mortgages.

Short computer programs can be written for hire purchase and mortgages.

3 Tax

How does the tax system work? Find out about rates of tax, allowances, etc. Making assumptions about your earnings and circumstances when you leave school work out how much tax you will have to pay.

Make suggestions for a less complicated system.

4 Local taxes

Find out about (a) rates, (b) community charges. Which is the fairer system? Compare the costs for various households.

How does your local council use the money it collects? How are schools, hospitals, etc. financed?

Make suggestions for a reform of the central government tax system and the local government system.

References

Leaflets from banks, building societies, post offices, etc. are a useful source. Many local councils produce leaflets showing how the money from rates is spent.

The Spode Group, *Solving Real Problems with CSE Mathematics* (Cranfield Press)

SMP, *New Book 5* (Cambridge University Press)

46 · Numbers and devices for calculation

In an age of calculators and computers it is easy to take numbers for granted. In fact the invention of our number system and the development of computational devices took a long time. This topic could be undertaken as a group project making a display to illustrate the historical development.

1 The development of number notation

The main stages which could be illustrated are:
(a) The fundamental number concept is that of one-to-one correspondence using stones, fingers, knotted ropes, tally sticks, etc. (The financial records of Great Britain were kept on tally sticks until 1826.) Some people in Papua New Guinea still use parts of their body for counting beyond ten.
(b) A later development was to record numbers using symbols. For example, about 4000 years ago the Babylonians recorded numbers on clay tablets by making marks with a wedge-shaped stick. The Romans used a finger-counting system: the symbol V for five comes from the shape of a hand and X comes from two hands.
(c) The *place value* system – in which the same symbol is used in different positions – was developed by the Hindus. To appreciate its advantages try to do a multiplication in Roman numbers – for example multiply CCXLIV by XXVII.
(d) The decimal point was introduced by the Scotsman John Napier in about 1600 but did not come into fully-accepted use until about 1750.

2 Pencil-and-paper methods

There was a need by merchants, for example, to devise efficient methods for doing computations rapidly. Some well-known methods for multiplication are
(a) 'Russian' multiplication (see *MMA*, activity 94)
(b) grid multiplication
(c) long multiplication (rapidly becoming an historical method)
and for subtraction:
(a) decomposition
(b) equal additions
(c) addition of the complement (see *MMA*, activity 93).

3 Devices

A display of computational devices, with explanations, could be made:
(a) Napier's bones   (b) nomograms
(c) slide rules   (d) logarithms
(e) mechanical calculators
(f) electronic calculators   (g) computers

References

Life Science Library, *Mathematics* (Time Life)
C. Boyer, *History of Mathematics* (Wiley)
SMP, *Book G* (Cambridge University Press)
T. Dantzig, *Number, the Language of Science* (Allen and Unwin)
B. Bolt, *More Mathematical Activities (MMA)* (Cambridge University Press)

47 ▪ The history of π

A study of the history of mathematics can serve to show that mathematics is a human activity which has developed over a period of time. The history of the number symbolised by π gives such an opportunity at an accessible level.

1 Circumference of a circle

How does the circumference of a circular object depend on its diameter? The circumference and diameter of various objects can be measured and the results presented graphically. It should be clear that the circumference is '3 and a bit' times the diameter.

Reference to 1 Kings 7:23 suggests that at that time the Jews took the multiplying factor to be 3.

2 Estimates for π

According to the Rhind Papyrus the Egyptians used $\frac{256}{81}$ for π. Hero of Alexandria (AD 75) used $3\frac{1}{7}$. Ptolemy (AD 150) used $3\frac{17}{120}$, which he wrote as $3°8'30''$ meaning $3 + \frac{8}{60} + \frac{30}{3600}$, effectively using a number base of 60.

The Hindus and the Chinese also had some close approximations:

$$\frac{49}{16}, \quad \sqrt{10}, \quad \frac{355}{113}.$$

The following short program (from *The Mathematical Gazette*, December 1983) gives rational approximations for π:

```
10 N = 0 : E = 1
20 N = N+1 : M = INT(N*PI+0.5)
30 F = ABS(M/N−PI)
40 IF F >= E THEN 20
50 E = F : PRINT M;"/";N: GOTO 20
```

The program gives a number of approximations very rapidly up to $\frac{355}{113}$. There is then a long pause (about 5 minutes) before the next approximations are printed.

3 Area

By drawing one square inside a circle and another outside it can be shown that the area of a circle of radius r is between $2r^2$ and $4r^2$.

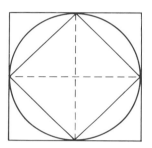

The method was extended by Archimedes who considered the limiting area of inscribed and circumscribed polygons. Details are given in Hogben's *Mathematics for the Million*.

A dissection model can be made to obtain the formula πr^2, knowing that the circumference is $2\pi r$. For details see SMP, *Book E Teacher's Guide*.

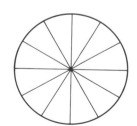

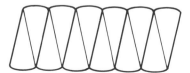

4 Series

The number symbolised by π occurs in situations unrelated to circles and can be obtained from various series:

(a) $\dfrac{\pi}{4} = \dfrac{1}{1} - \dfrac{1}{3} + \dfrac{1}{5} - \dfrac{1}{7} + \cdots$

(b) $\dfrac{\pi^2}{6} = \dfrac{1}{1^2} + \dfrac{1}{2^2} + \dfrac{1}{3^2} + \dfrac{1}{4^2} + \cdots$

(c) $\dfrac{\pi^4}{90} = \dfrac{1}{1^4} + \dfrac{1}{2^4} + \dfrac{1}{3^4} + \dfrac{1}{4^4} + \cdots$

(d) $\dfrac{\pi^8}{9450} = \dfrac{1}{1^8} + \dfrac{1}{2^8} + \dfrac{1}{3^8} + \dfrac{1}{4^8} + \cdots$

The first converges very slowly, the fourth extremely rapidly.

Wallis (1656) obtained the product

$$\dfrac{\pi}{2} = \dfrac{2}{1} \times \dfrac{2}{3} \times \dfrac{4}{3} \times \dfrac{4}{5} \times \dfrac{6}{5} \times \dfrac{6}{7} \times \dfrac{8}{7} \times \cdots$$

Short computer programs can be written to obtain approximations for π from these series.

Using computers π has been determined to many thousands of decimal places. Mathematicians are interested to see if there is a pattern in the digits.

References

L. Hogben, *Mathematics for the Million* (Pan)

SMP, *Book E Teacher's Guide* (Cambridge University Press)

B. Bolt, *More Mathematical Activities* (Cambridge University Press)

R. Courant and H. Robbins, *What is Mathematics?* (Oxford University Press)

C. Boyer, *A History of Mathematics* (Wiley)

5 Probability

(a) *Buffon's needle.* It was shown by Buffon (1777) that when a needle of length l is thrown on a set of parallel lines, distance d apart, the probability that the needle crosses a line is $\dfrac{2l}{\pi d}$.

By carrying out the experiment a large number of times an approximation for π can be obtained. It is convenient to make l about $\tfrac{3}{4}d$ so that the probability is about $\tfrac{1}{2}$.

(b) *Monte Carlo method.* A random point is chosen in the square. The probability it is in the quadrant of the circle is

$$\dfrac{\text{area of quadrant}}{\text{area of square}} = \dfrac{\pi}{4}.$$

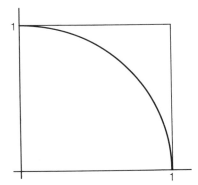

A computer program can be written to find an approximation to π using this method. It is necessary to generate two random decimals, x and y, find if the point determined by them is in the quadrant (using $x^2 + y^2 < 1$); and repeat many times. The fraction of the points in the quadrant is then an approximation for $\dfrac{\pi}{4}$.

48 ▪ Pythagoras' theorem

Pythagoras' theorem is usually applied to calculate the length of one side of a right-angled triangle given the lengths of the other two sides. In its original form it was a result about areas of squares. The construction of models to demonstrate the area property makes an interesting project. A classroom display could be made of various demonstrations.

1 A particular case of Pythagoras' theorem can often be seen in fabrics, wall-papers, tiles, etc. Collect examples.

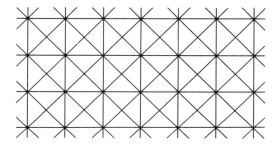

2 The following method is attributed to the Hindu mathematician Bhaskara (about AD 1150). He did not feel that the method needed any explanation: he just wrote 'Behold!' underneath it.

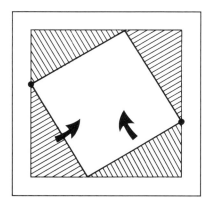 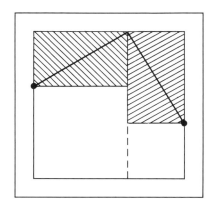

A model can be made using a piece of softboard (as used for noticeboards), coloured card and pins.

3 Another well-known dissection is due to Perigal. (See *MA*, activity 64.) The second largest square is split up by first finding its centre (by drawing the diagonals) and then lines are drawn parallel to and perpendicular to the hypotenuse of the triangle.

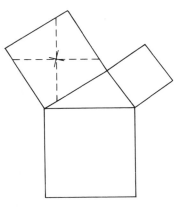 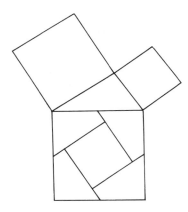

4 An attractive demonstration can be made using two pieces of heavy card: A is joined to B and C is joined to D by shirring elastic. The pieces are held, one in each hand, and then the piece on the right is turned over to give the position shown in the second diagram.

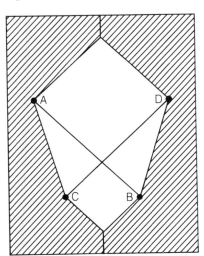 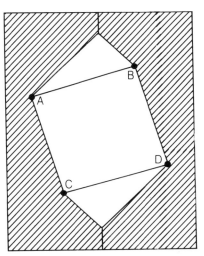

5 A range of alternative proofs of Pythagoras' theorem are discussed in *EMMA*, activity 60.

References

SMP, *Book E* (Cambridge University Press)
B. Bolt, *Mathematical Activities (MA)*, and *Even More Mathematical Activities (EMMA)* (Cambridge University Press)

49 ▪ Calculating prodigies

Some people have a remarkable facility for doing complicated calculations very rapidly in their heads. Although in the age of electronic calculators this is not a particularly *useful* skill it does have a fascination, and some pupils might be interested in finding out about the methods used by these prodigies and learning some techniques themselves.

1 Some fast human calculators

One famous 'lightning calculator' was George Bidder, born in 1806 at Moretonhampstead in Devon. As a boy he was taken around the country by his father to give demonstrations of his ability at mental calculation. His father made a lot of money by exhibiting his son, but eventually he was persuaded to allow George to go to university. George became an engineer designing railways and the Victoria Docks in London.

George was able to see numbers as patterns. For example, he visualised 984 as a rectangular array of dots, 24 lines of 41 dots. To find 173 × 397 he thought of a picture like this:

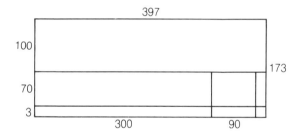

Then he did

100 × 397 =	39 700	
70 × 300 =	21 000	60 700
70 × 90 =	6 300	67 000
70 × 7 =	490	67 490
3 × 300 =	900	68 390
3 × 90 =	270	68 660
3 × 7 =	21	68 681

In 1978 the Indian lady Mrs Shakuntala Devi appeared on the Blue Peter programme on BBC television and did calculations such as

     Multiply 637 432 by 513 124

and   Find the cube root of 71 991 296

in a couple of seconds.

2 How to calculate quickly

There are some easily applied methods for doing rapid calculations.

(a) George Bidder's method of multiplication can be applied to multiplication of two-digit numbers.

For example, to do 27×43 think of it as the area of a floor measuring 27 m by 43 m. The areas of the four rectangles can then be added mentally.

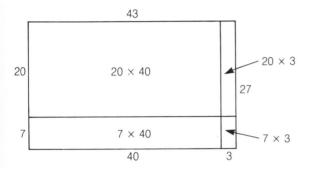

(b) A quick method to square a two-digit number with 5 as a units digit is to add 1 to the tens digit, multiply the result by the tens digit and follow it with 25.

For example, $75^2 \rightarrow 8 \times 7 = 56 \rightarrow 5625$

(c) A quick method to multiply by 11 is to write down the units digit, then add the units digit to the tens digit, the tens digit to the hundreds digit and so on, finishing with the final digit.

For example, 152×11

Write down the units digit	2
2 add 5 is 7	72
5 add 1 is 6	672
Write down the final digit	1672

(d) By memorising the cubes of numbers from 1 to 10, cube roots of numbers can be found.

Number	1	2	3	4	5	6
Cube	1	8	27	64	125	216

Number	7	8	9	10
Cube	343	512	729	1000

Ask someone to secretly choose a number from 1 to 100 and cube it. Suppose the result is 571 787. The units digit is 7. Reading from cube to number they must have chosen a number with a units digit of 3.

Ignore the last three digits and look at 571. It lies between the cubes of 8 and 9. Hence the number must have been 83.

(e) Explain the quick methods and develop some more. For example, find quick ways for 462×50, 360×125, $2125 \div 25$.

References

W. W. Rouse Ball, *Mathematical Recreations and Essays* (Macmillan)
M. Gardner, *Mathematical Carnival* (Penguin)
The Trachtenberg Speed System (Pan)
Blue Peter, *Fourteenth Annual* (BBC)

50 · Traffic

'This road is dangerous. The traffic goes far too fast.' Such statements are frequently made about the traffic in a town or village. There might be a campaign for an alternative route or for a pedestrian crossing. Such campaigns need evidence. Various projects can be carried out on this theme and can be presented as reports to a newspaper or to a local council.

1 Speed

How fast do vehicles travel?

To find the speeds of vehicles it is helpful to mark out two points a known distance apart – for example, 100 metres or 100 yards. The vehicles can be timed over this distance with a stopwatch. Knowing the distance and the time, the speed can then be found using a calculator or by reading from a pre-drawn graph of time (for 100 metres) – speed.

A decision will need to be taken as to whether metric or imperial units should be used. There is opportunity here for getting a feel for metric units – for example, what is 30 miles per hour in metres per second? A conversion graph could be made.

2 Traffic density

What is the traffic density (i.e. how many vehicles are there in a 100 metre length, say)? How does it depend on the time of day and the day of the week?

One method to determine the traffic density is to mark out a length of 100 metres, say. Then, standing at the 'top' end, note the vehicle passing the 'lower' end and count the vehicles passing until the one noted comes by.

3 Rate of flow

What is the rate of flow (i.e. how many vehicles pass per time interval, for example, per minute)? How does it depend on the time of day and the day of the week?

4 Composition of the traffic

What fraction consists of lorries? Cars? Motorcycles? Bicycles? Etc. How many people are there in each car? What fraction of the cars contain just one person?

5 Crossing the road

How long do people have to wait to cross the road? How long does it take to cross (especially elderly people and young children)? Is a pedestrian crossing needed?

6 Noise

Measure the noise levels on the road and in houses using a sound-level meter (possibly obtainable from the science department).

References

Local libraries, information centres, road safety offices, newspapers

51 ▪ Public transport

Public transport is frequently in the news. Statements in the press such as the one below can form the basis of a project on the local public transport system.

1 Punctuality

Do trains (or buses) in your locality run on time?

Pupils who live near a train or bus station could check the times of arrival and departure, or, if there is a bus stop near home or school, the times of arrival could be checked.

Does punctuality depend on the day of the week? On the time of day?

A report could be written in a form which could be submitted to a local newspaper or to the bus or train company.

40% of expresses were late

Nearly half British Rail's express trains and a quarter of all commuter trains arrived late last year, the rail users' watchdog body said in its annual report yesterday.

2 The size of buses

In 1984 an experimental urban minibus project was set up in Exeter. Conventional buses were replaced by minibuses running a high frequency 'hail and stop' service.

What are the advantages and disadvantages of replacing large buses by minibuses? Consider the economics of such a system. Write a report about it.

3 The use of public transport

How full are buses and trains? What usage needs to be made of a particular service for it to 'break even'? Why do people use public transport? What would encourage people to use it more?

References

Bus and train timetables

52 . The flow of traffic around a roundabout

Traffic roundabouts have been designed to ease the flow of traffic at busy junctions without the need of traffic lights or a policeman on point duty. A study of a local roundabout at a busy period to analyse the traffic flows and then a simulation model of the situation would make an excellent project.

1 Analysis of traffic flow

(a) Traffic counts for 10 minute periods of the number of vehicles arriving at each junction would give an estimate of the flow in vehicles an hour.
(b) What happens to each vehicle is difficult to follow once it enters the roundabout but the proportion of vehicles on an arc of a roundabout which leave at the next junction would be a useful statistic.
(c) What gap in traffic on the roundabout is needed before a car can enter the roundabout from a feeder road?

2 Simulation of traffic flow

Working for example in 1 second steps, random numbers could be used to give the arrival of cars at the roundabout. Suppose 1200 cars an hour arrive at one particular junction, which represents on average 1 car every 3 seconds; this could be simulated by tossing a dice where scores of 1 and 2 represent the arrival of a car, while scores of 3, 4, 5 and 6 indicate no car has arrived. The arrival of cars at each junction will have to be similarly simulated and then what happens to these cars in successive seconds will need to be carefully recorded.

3 Formation of queues

Investigate the effect of different traffic flows on the build up of queues, and outflow along the feeder roads.

4 Computer simulation

Write a computer program to simulate traffic flow on a roundabout.

References

SMP 11–16, *Book YE2* (Cambridge University Press)
Local council highways department

53 · Traffic lights

Traffic lights are frequently used at busy road junctions or to operate single lane flow at roadworks to avoid accidents, but they do mean that traffic is halted for more than one half of the time in at least one direction. An analysis of the operation of traffic lights has possibilities for a variety of projects.

1 Investigate the use of traffic lights at a local crossroads.
(a) Note carefully the time spent with the lights in each phase of the operation and when the lights in one direction change relative to the lights in the other direction.
(b) For what time are both sets of light red together?
(c) Is the green phase the same length of time in both directions?
(d) How long is a complete sequence and how many cars can hope to cross in both directions in one sequence?

2 Use random number tables or dice or a microcomputer to simulate different traffic flows to see at what level of traffic flow queues would be expected to build beyond the number able to cross in one green phase.

3 Where a minor road crosses a major road the lights are sometimes arranged to be green for the major road traffic unless a car arrives on the minor road. Investigate how this operates.

4 When a road is being dug up to lay a pipe the traffic flow is often restricted to one lane and controlled by temporary traffic lights at each end. Model a suitable sequencing of the lights taking into account
(a) the distance between the lights,
(b) the speed at which traffic would travel between the lights,
(c) different flows of traffic in opposite directions.

5 Design a mechanical rotary switch which would operate the lights, in sequence, on a typical crossroads.

6 Design a computer program and display to simulate the operation of a typical set of traffic lights.

References

SMP 11–16, *Book YE2* (Cambridge University Press)

54 • Stopping distances

Speed (m.p.h.)	30	40	50	60	70
Thinking distance (ft)	30	40	50	60	70
(m)	9	12	15	18	21
Braking distance (ft)	45	80	125	180	245
(m)	14	24	38	55	75
Stopping distance (ft)	75	120	175	240	315
(m)	23	36	53	73	96

To pass a driving test a learner driver needs to know the Highway Code. Included in this are the approximate stopping distances for a car being driven in good conditions on a dry road. This makes a good starting point for a project.

1 With the same set of axes graphs can be drawn to show the thinking, braking and stopping distances in feet or metres against the speed of a car in m.p.h. The graphs might also be shown as bar charts with the bars in two colours to indicate which part represents the thinking distance and which the braking distance.

2 Show that the stopping distance (S ft) and the speed (V m.p.h.) are related by the formula

$$S = V + \frac{1}{20}V^2$$

Use the formula or a graph to estimate the stopping distances for speeds other than those given in the table.

There is no simple formula relating the stopping distance in metres to the speed in m.p.h. But the Highway Code suggests a simple rule in good conditions is to leave a gap of one metre for each m.p.h. of your speed.

Draw a graph to represent this on top of a graph showing the stopping distance in metres and discuss the differences.

3 The Ministry of Transport Manual, *Driving*, recommends that the stopping distances in poor conditions should be amended in the table to 150 ft, 240 ft, 350 ft, 480 ft and 630 ft. What would be the appropriate formula?

4 How good are drivers at estimating the distances given in the table? Test this on a variety of people by
(a) asking them the distance of an object that you have placed say 60 m away,
(b) having a number of flags at measured intervals and ask for the distances between them.
  Are experienced drivers better than non-drivers?
  Does age or sex make any difference?
  Does a person's ability to estimate distance differ along a road as compared to being in an open space?

5 60 m.p.h. is about 90 feet per second. The MOT model for the thinking distance assumes that a person driving a car at this speed will have travelled 60 feet before reacting to a situation and applying the brakes. What does this assume about the driver's reaction time? Construct an experiment to measure a person's reaction time. How will it change if a radio is playing or the person is in conversation?
  How would the MOT model differ if the reaction time was assumed to be 0.5 seconds or 1.0 second say?

6 Cooperate with a friend who has a bicycle with a speedometer and do a series of experiments to find the stopping distance of a bicycle at different speeds. What would be the results if (a) just the front brake, (b) just the rear brake was used?

How do the results differ when the roads are wet?

7 What is the capacity of a single lane on a motorway if the traffic is all travelling along the road at V m.p.h. leaving a space between vehicles equivalent to that recommended in the Highway Code? Investigate the optimum speed for the largest number of vehicles an hour which can safely travel along the motorway.

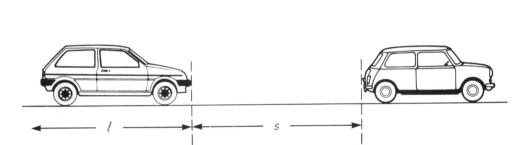

Vm.p.h

8 When temporary traffic lights are in use for road repairs where should the warning notices be placed and for what distance should the lights be visible for oncoming cars?

How long does it take a car to come to a halt from 50 m.p.h.? How long should the amber signal last?

9 Investigate the stopping distances of (a) a person running, (b) a train, (c) an oil tanker, (d) a jumbo jet on the runway. Where is such information used?

References

The Highway Code

The Ministry of Transport Manual: *Driving* (HMSO)

The Spode Group, *Solving Real Problems with Mathematics* (Cranfield Press)

55 · Car parking

As the number of people who rely on cars as their main means of transport increases there are increasing problems for parking in towns and places of work. Several ideas are given for analysing how parking is provided in a locality and ways in which it might be improved.

1 How many cars can reasonably be expected to park along a 100 metre stretch of road?

Measurements will need to be made of the lengths of typical cars and of the distances left between them for ease of parking. An interesting comparison could be made with the distance between parking meters where they are used.

2 Make a study of a local ground-level car park and note how the bays are marked, or how drivers park if no bays are marked.

How much space needs to be left to allow doors to open?

How much space needs to be allowed between rows for access?

How does the turning circle of a car influence the space needed?

Another possibility is to investigate how much space a disabled driver using a wheelchair will need, and check if the parking bays for disabled people allow for this.

3 In what ways do short-stay car parks such as those associated with shopping centres and motorway service stations need to be different from long-stay parks associated with places of work?

Why can cars be packed very close together on a ferry or at a park for a football match? Compare the efficiency of such parking with that of a short-stay park.

4 Survey a school playground or other suitable piece of land and show how to mark it out as a car park.

5 Design a multi-storey car park for an urban shopping area capable of holding 400 cars. Give plans, elevations and a scale model.

6 How many cars, on average, use the car park in your local shopping centre in a day, in a week?

7 What annual income can a local authority expect to get from its car parks?

References

The Spode Group, *Solving Real Problems with Mathematics, Vol. 2* (Cranfield Press)

56 . Buying and running your own transport

Many fourteen- and fifteen-year-olds are looking ahead to the time when they can have a vehicle of their own. There are various possibilities for projects on this topic which capitalise on their natural interest.

1 Running cost

How much does it cost to keep a moped, motorbike or car?

A particular make and model which the pupil would like to own could be chosen or their parents' car could be used.

Some points to consider:
- depreciation (see section 2)
- insurance
- road tax
- petrol
- maintenance
- MOT test

2 Buying cost

Is it better to buy new or second-hand cars? How do cars depreciate?

Compare different makes and models. It might be useful to draw graphs and to calculate percentages, etc.

Books giving second-hand car prices are published monthly and are obtainable from newsagents and bookshops. Alternatively, prices from advertisements in a local paper could be used.

3 Length of life

How long do cars last? What is the average age of cars? Do some makes last longer than others?

The approximate age of cars can be deduced from their registration number (except for very old cars and for those with personalised registrations). When conducting a survey some thought will need to be given to the elimination of bias – for example, would the school car park be a suitable place to conduct a survey?

A comparison could be made between the ages of teachers' cars and the ages of cars in an office car park, say.

4 Mileage

What is the average yearly distance travelled by cars?

This could be estimated by carrying out, with permission, a survey of parked cars, recording their age (determined by the registration number) and the distance shown on the mileometer.

Some points for discussion:
- The average yearly distance for 'young' cars will be unreliable.
- Some older cars might be 'second time round' on their mileometer.
- People such as sales representatives often do a large mileage on 'young' cars.

5 Popularity

What is the most popular colour for cars? What is the most popular make of car? What fraction of cars are of foreign manufacture?

References

Books of second-hand car prices, for example, *Exchange and Mart Guide to Buying Your Second-hand Car*, *Parker's Car Price Guide*
The Spode Group, *Solving Real Problems with CSE Mathematics* (Cranfield Press)

57 ▪ Canals and waterways

Before the advent of the railways the canals were the main means of heavy transport. There still remains a complex network of canals across the countryside left from this era but it is now used mainly for pleasure cruising. Many of the design problems solved by the canal engineers were later used in building the railways and more recently the motorways, but some problems were specific to canals. The idea of this topic for a project is to consider some of the mathematics associated with the working and building of a canal.

1 Where possible canals avoided locks by using cuttings, embankments, contouring and even tunnels. They were built at a time when all the earth moved had to be with a pick, shovel and wheelbarrow. Survey an embankment or cutting and try to estimate its volume in wheelbarrow loads. Engineers try to arrange the route so that the volume of 'cut' balances the amount of 'fill'. Can you find evidence of this?

2 Calculate the volume of water in a lock when full. Every time a lock is used this volume flows downstream. Investigate the source of water at the head of the canal and compute the flow required for a given number of boats passing through the lock in an hour. You should be able to see why some canals become almost unusable in a dry period.

3 Investigate journey times along a canal. Try to produce a formula for the time between points d miles apart and passing through n locks.

4 By estimating the displacement of a narrow boat or barge when empty and when full calculate the tonnage it can carry.

References

A. Burton, *Canals in Colour* (Blandford)

58 ▪ The water supply

Until there is a prolonged drought or a burst water main most city dwellers take for granted a ready supply of water. This is only made possible by planners forecasting the future needs of a population on the one hand and the engineers building reservoirs to store a sufficient volume of water on the other.

1 A recent statistic suggests that the average US city dweller needs about 125 US gallons* of water a day. How is all this used?

Investigate the volume of water used by your household in a typical week. How much water is used in: flushing the toilet, having a bath, having a shower, cleaning teeth, washing the dishes, washing the clothes, cleaning the car, watering the garden? How much do you drink? How much is used in cooking and cleaning vegetables?

2 Try to estimate the total daily water requirement of your locality. Industrial users and farmers need special consideration.

3 How does the water demand of a town vary through a typical day? Consider the varying demands of a holiday region in and out of season.

The South West Water Authority reckons to supply its resident population of 1.4 million about 100 million gallons of fresh drinking water daily. However in the peak holiday months the population increases to 2 million at a time when gardeners and farmers use more water for irrigation.

4 Estimate the volume of water your local authority would need to store to allow for a six week drought and compare this with the capacity of your nearest reservoir.

5 See if there are any suitable valley sites in your area which could be dammed to form a reservoir. Study the catchment area and rainfall figures for one of these and design a reservoir. A model of the valley and dam would be appropriate with details of the volume of water it would contain for varying depths.

6 In an area with bore holes how large do the reservoirs need to be? Why do some areas have water towers, and what decides their capacity?

References

The local water authority
Life Science Library: *Water* (Time Life)

*125 US gallons is equivalent to about 105 UK (imperial) gallons or 475 litres.

59 ▪ The milk supply

A consideration of where all the milk comes from, how it is collected, processed, packaged and distributed gives plenty of material for a range of projects.

1 Where does the milk come from?

How much milk is obtained from a typical cow annually?

How does the milk yield vary through the year?

How does the milk yield vary with the breed of cow?

How does the milk yield depend on how a cow is fed and what are the economics of increasing output at the expense of costly concentrates?

2 The geographical distribution of the human population differs from that of the herds of milking cows.

Large milk tankers drive from farm to farm in rural areas collecting the milk. See what you can find out about the routes they take and the timetable on which they operate.

How many tankers does the creamery operate and how long a time elapses between the cows being milked and the milk being pasturised?

3 From where does your local dairy get its milk?

How long does it take from a cow being milked to the milk being delivered at your door?

Find out about the routes used by the milk deliverers in your area. How many households do they expect to visit on a round? How many pints/litres of milk can they carry on their milk float?

What is the average milk order per household and how long does it take to deliver?

How does a delivery time differ when money has to be collected and how is this managed?

How do milk orders differ from household to household and through the week and how does the delivery man record this?

4 Where milk bottles are used find out about their initial costs, average length of life, collection costs and cleaning costs and compare this with the costs of disposable cartons.

5 Compare the price of milk at the door to that paid to the farmer and see whether the difference is justified.

6 Milk deliveries are now often only made viable by roundsmen selling fruit juice, bread, eggs and other foods. Investigate the economics of this.

References

The local dairy, creamery and farmer where appropriate; the Milk Marketing Board

60 ▪ The postal service

The collection, sorting, distribution and delivery of mail is a very complex process which we so easily take for granted. Many aspects of this process can be investigated and be used as the basis of projects.

1 Postal collection

Locate all the post boxes in your area and decide the greatest distance anyone has to travel to post a letter.

What is (a) the mean, (b) the median distances of households from letter boxes?

Decide on some criteria such as 'no-one shall be more than 400 m from a post box' and see where you would place the post boxes in your locality.

Investigate the routes taken by mail vans in collecting the mail from the boxes. Can you find a more efficient scheme?

2 How many letters are posted?

Where do all the letters come from? Which kinds of organisations generate most mail? How many letters/cards are posted by your household in a typical week?

At what times of the day/week/year does most posting take place?

What proportion of mail is (a) local, (b) first class, (c) overseas?

3 Sorting and distribution

How is the mail sorted? Is it done in stages? How do postal codes work?

How long does a letter spend in a sorting office?

How does a first-class letter manage to get to anywhere else in the country in a day?

How is the main distribution network organised?

4 Delivery

How many postmen are required in a town of 40 000 people for the usual morning delivery? How many places can a postman visit in an urban area compared to a rural area or in a close packed housing estate compared to a leafy, spacious suburb?

Is it quicker for a postman to deliver to the houses on one side of a street and then the other or to keep crossing from one side to the other? Investigate the conditions under which one would be better than the other.

5 Postal charges and stamps

(a) Consider the postal rates for letters and parcels and draw step graphs to represent the postage against the weight.

(b) Stamp books are issued from machines outside most post offices so that for a 50p coin a person can purchase a selection of stamps to post a letter when the office is shut. How are the values of the stamps arranged to allow the best use of the stamps for first and second class mail? (See, for example, *EMMA*, activities 50 and 51).

(c) Design a book of eight stamps to be used in a machine taking a £1 coin when the first and second class postage rates are 18p and 13p respectively.

6 How long does a letter take to reach its destination?

When are the best and worst times for posting?

How long does a letter spend

(a) in the postbox?
(b) in the mail van after collection?
(c) in the sorting office?
(d) travelling between distribution centres?
(e) being delivered?

How might the service be improved?

7 Parcel post

(a) What are the differences in charges/delivery times between parcel post and letter post? When would it be better to send a small parcel by letter post than parcel post?

(b) The Post Office states that for sending parcels through the post their maximum length must not exceed 1.070 m whilst the sum of the length and circumference of the cross-section perpendicular to this length must not exceed 2.000 m. Investigate different cuboid shapes which could be sent and find the one with maximum volume. Show that a cylinder could be sent which contained a larger volume. How about a sphere? What would be the length of the longest, thin, metal rod which could be sent?

References

Any post office and sorting office

B. Bolt, *Even More Mathematical Activities (EMMA)* (Cambridge University Press)

The Spode Group, *Solving Real Problems with CSE Mathematics* (Cranfield Press)

61 ▪ Telephone charges

The arrival of a telephone bill is often followed by recriminations about who has been spending too long on the phone. Trying to get behind a household's quarterly bill and looking at the relative costs of phoning at different times of the day and to different destinations makes a good self-contained project.

Time allowances for each unit (in seconds): Local and National	Cheap Rate Mon–Fri 6pm–8am Sat & Sun all day	Standard Rate Mon–Fri 8am–9am 1pm–6pm	Peak Rate Mon–Fri 9am–1pm
Local: up to 32 km (20 miles)	360	90	60
National rate a: up to 56 km (35 miles)	100	34.3	25.7
National rate b1: low cost over 56 km	60	30	22.5
National rate b: over 56 km	45	24	18

1 Make an analysis of the people in your house who use the phone and the people they contact. Use a map and your telephone directory to determine at which rate (L, a, b) the calls will be charged. Further, use the information given out by British Telecom to see if any of the b rated calls use one of the 146 special low-cost routes which link major towns and cities and so are chargeable at the b1 rate.

2 Over a period of some time make an analysis of who uses your phone, at what time of day, for how long and who they phone. Note that incoming calls can be ignored, unless the caller is reversing the charge!

3 Use the information you have collected together with the current unit charge (4.4p plus 15% VAT in 1987) to estimate your quarterly bill. You will also need to add on the quarterly rental for the line and telephone.

4 Compare your estimate with the actual bill and make recommendations to your family on how to reduce future bills. It is now possible to buy a phone and reduce rental charges. Compare the costs of renting and buying a telephone and include this in your recommendations.

References

Telephone directory, British Telecom

62 ▪ Waste disposal

Most of us take for granted the disposal of all our domestic rubbish unless there is a strike of refuse collectors, when the waste materials seem to accumulate at an alarming rate. Here are several ideas for projects which investigate the volume of domestic waste produced in a locality, and its disposal.

1 Consider the range of containers used to temporarily store waste and their relative volumes: waste paper bin, kitchen bin, domestic refuse bins, mini skips, large skips, refuse lorries.

2 Investigate the volume and/or mass of rubbish put out by the average household for collection each week. What proportion of the waste is plastic, metal, paper?

3 Consider the collection of the waste. How many dustbins can one refuse collector empty in an hour? How many men operate one refuse disposal lorry and how many full dustbins will the lorry take before it needs to be tipped? How long is the lorry out of circulation while it visits the tip? In your locality how many lorries and refuse collectors are needed to deal with the weekly refuse?

4 How are the collection routes organised? Try to devise an alternative, better, system.

5 Estimate the annual cost of refuse disposal and compare this with the charge on the rates.

6 Investigate the economics of bottle banks.

7 Consider the cost of collecting waste paper separately and the income which might be made by selling it to paper mills for reprocessing.

8 Consider the operation of a skip contractor.

References

Local authority engineering department, waste disposal
Local library information centre
Skip hire – see *Yellow Pages* telephone directory

63 ■ Triangular frameworks

Engineers have known for a long time that whenever they need a light, strong, rigid structure they cannot do better than use a framework of triangles. It is suggested here that a project is based on investigating ways of making two- and three-dimensional frameworks rigid and relating this to applications in the real world.

1 Making polygonal frameworks rigid

Use card strips or plastic strips joined by paper fasteners to investigate ways to make a polygonal framework rigid. This diagram illustrates, for example, six ways of making an hexagonal framework rigid by using just three diagonal struts. In general it will be found that a polygonal framework with n sides can always be made rigid using $n-3$ diagonal struts. Investigate ways of making a framework rigid where the additional struts join the mid-points or some other points of the sides.

2 Finding examples of triangular structures

Look out for examples of the triangle framework in everyday use such as shelf brackets, diagonal bars on gates, cycle frames, roof structures, ironing board legs, window opening fastenings, rotary clothes lines, umbrellas, deck chairs, music stands, scaffolding, boat rigging etc., and record them.

A good source of light rigid frameworks is a fun fair; for example, the big wheel relies on the triangle for strength.

3 Three-dimensional structures

Many bridges are outstanding examples of the use of triangular frameworks in three dimensions. The Connell Ferry, Forth, Sydney Harbour and Quebec bridges are just a few around the world which have stood the test of time. In these structures the triangles fit together into interlocking tetrahedrons which are exceptionally strong.

(a) Make a tetrahedron by threading shirring elastic (or thread) through drinking straws and tying the ends at the corners. Other polyhedra frameworks such as the octahedron and icosahedron, whose faces are all triangles, are also rigid, but the cube is not. To make the cube rigid you will need to put a diagonal strut in each of its six faces, see below.

See what other rigid three-dimensional structures you can make using straws and shirring elastic.

(b) Take a close look at a tall crane which swings overhead on a building site and try to analyse the structure of its mast and jib. Make a straw model of the jib.

(c) Electricity pylons are excellent examples of triangular structures, as are television transmission masts and the Eiffel Tower. Make a model of one of them.

(d) A modern use of the triangle is seen in the geodesic domes invented by the American genius Buckminster Fuller for covering sports arenas, or on a smaller scale as greenhouses and climbing frames, while the microlight planes and the undercarriage of the lunar space module use the essential rigidity of the triangular structure. Collect pictures or make drawings of these towards a scrap book on rigid structures.

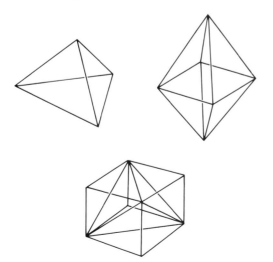

References

B. Bolt, *More Mathematical Activities*, activities 44 and 45 (Cambridge University Press)

The Buckminster Fuller Reader (Penguin)

R. Buckminster Fuller, *Synergetics* (Macmillan)

D. Beckett, *Brunel's Britain* (David and Charles)

D. Goldwater, *Bridges and How They are Built* (World's Work Ltd)

E. de Maré, *Bridges of Britain* (Batsford)

J. E. Gordon, *Structures* (Penguin)

K. Shooter and J. Saxton, *Making Things Work: An Introduction to Design Technology* (Cambridge University Press)

64 ▪ Four-bar linkages

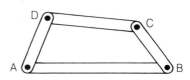

One of the commonest components of a mechanism is a four-bar linkage which, in its simplest form, can be thought of as four bars pivoted at their ends to form a quadrilateral ABCD as shown. If one bar of this linkage is fixed then the movement of the other three is determined by what happens to any one of them. How, where and why this linkage is used makes for a fascinating project involving motion geometry in the real world.

To make up linkages for this project you will need to cut up some thick card into strips and have a good supply of paper fasteners, or if available use geostrips or Meccano.

1 Parallelogram linkages

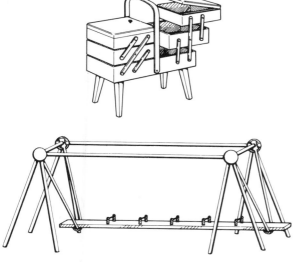

When AB = CD and AD = BC the linkages form a *parallelogram* and will always move keeping the opposite sides parallel. This property is used in countless situations such as in: a needlework box, a children's swing, the windscreen wiper mounting on many coaches, letter scales and chemical balances, lift bridges and venetian blinds to name but a few. See what other examples you can find, record them and make working models to illustrate how they move (see *MA*, activity 51).

2 Trapezium linkages

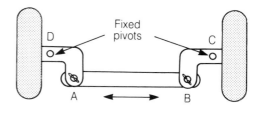

When AD = BC but AB ≠ DC then the *trapezium* linkage formed has many significant applications. It is used:
(a) to provide the rocking horse motion;
(b) to keep the front wheels of a car correctly aligned;
(c) to provide a good approximation to straight line motion, and forms the basis of designs by James Watt 1784, Tchebycheff 1850 and Roberts 1860.

See *MA*, activities 52, 53 and 54, and also *MMA*, activity 10.

3 Oscillating motion

In many mechanisms a constant speed motor causes another part of the mechanism to oscillate to and fro as on a windscreen wiper or in the agitator in a washing machine. This is often achieved by a four-bar linkage as shown here where AD makes complete revolutions about A and forces BC to oscillate about B.

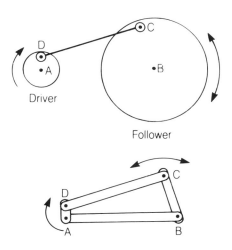

Driver

Follower

Investigate the angle of oscillation of BC for different ratios of the length of BC to AD.

This is also the mechanism of a treadle or of a cyclist when pedalling except that in these cases BC is the driver and AD the follower. See *EMMA*, activity 34.

4 Interlocking four-bar linkages

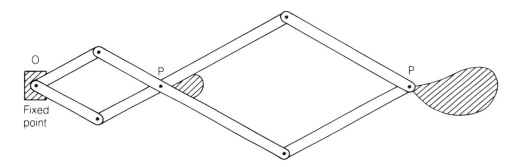

O

Fixed point

P

P

(a) Interlocking four-bar linkages can be used to enlarge a drawing or a map. The pantograph is one example. Another is shown here which enlarges with a linear scale factor of 3 from O.

Design other linkages which do the same.

See *MA*, activity 55, and *Machines, Mechanisms and Mathematics*.

(b) Many folding structures such as pushchairs, folding beds and clothes airers rely on interlocking linkages. See what you can discover. Analyse the mechanisms and try to model them.

References

B. Bolt, *Mathematical Activities (MA)*, *More Mathematical Activities (MMA)*, and *Even More Mathematical Activities (EMMA)* (Cambridge University Press)

Schools Council, Mathematics for the Majority Project, *Machines, Mechanisms and Mathematics* by B. Bolt and J. Hiscocks (Chatto and Windus)

S. Strandh, *Machines, An Illustrated History* (Nordbok)

S. Molian, *Mechanism Design* (Cambridge University Press)

D. Lent, *Analysis and Design of Mechanisms* (Prentice Hall)

K. Shooter and J. Saxton, *Making Things Work: An Introduction to Design Technology* (Cambridge University Press)

65 ▪ Parabolic reflectors

The curve known as a parabola has a very special point associated with it, the *focus*. If lines are drawn from the focus until they meet the curve and reflect off the curve as if it was a curved mirror then the reflected lines will all be in the same direction, parallel to the axis of symmetry of the parabola. This property has made parabolic reflectors of great importance and forms the basis of a very interesting project.

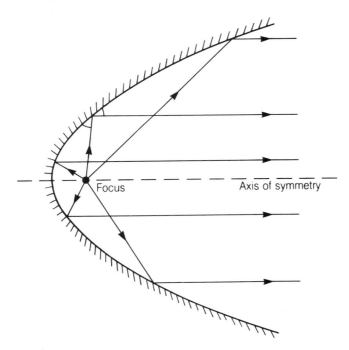

Focus   Axis of symmetry

1 Drawing a parabola

Investigate different ways of drawing a parabola:
(a) Graph $y = kx^2$ for different k (a microcomputer would help).
(b) Use the intersections of a family of parallel lines and a family of concentric circles.
(c) Use a set square touching a fixed point and a fixed line.
(d) Use the stitched curve approach.
    (See *MMA*, activity 71.)

2 Finding the focus

Find out how to determine the position of the focus of a parabola; for example, by drawing lines parallel to its axis and estimating the way they would reflect off the curve. Note that the focus of $y = kx^2$ is at $(0, \frac{1}{4}k)$.

Where is the focus of the parabolas produced by methods (b) and (c)?

3 Parabolic reflectors in use

Find as many examples as you can of parabolic reflectors in use. In many, the source of energy is put at the focus and sent out as a parallel beam such as in a torch, spotlight, electric bar fire. In others the reflector is used to focus the energy from a distant source such as radar aerials, parabolic reflectors for receiving television signals from satellites, telescopes such as that at Mount Palomar with a 200 inch diameter parabolic mirror which can collect 1 000 000 times as much light as a human eye. Large astronomical telescopes are also parabolic such as that at Jodrell Bank.

What happens if a source of light is moved away from the focus of a parabolic reflector? Experiment with a torch whose bulb can be screwed in and out.

How does a car 'dip' its headlights?

How do naturalists record bird song?

Why are the rear walls of some band stands built in the shape of a parabola?

4 Solar ovens

Scientists have experimented for many years with ways of converting the sun's energy into a usable form. At the turn of this century an experiment in Egypt used parabolic reflectors to produce enough steam to drive a 100 horsepower steam engine. More recently French and American scientists have used parabolic reflectors to produce large solar furnaces capable of producing temperatures in excess of 4400 °C.

Make a small solar oven using metal foil as the reflecting surface and heat up a test tube of water or burn a hole in a piece of paper at its focus.

References

B. Bolt, *More Mathematical Activities (MMA)* (Cambridge University Press)

E. H. Lockwood, *A Book of Curves* (Cambridge University Press)

How Things Work, Vol. 1 (Paladin)

Life Science Library: *Sound and Hearing*, and *Energy* (Time Life)

66 ▪ How effective is a teacosy?

Many people like their tea or coffee to be as hot as possible while others prefer to let their drinks cool before drinking. The object of this project is to investigate the rate at which liquids cool under differing conditions.

1 Boil a kettle of water and take its temperature at two minute intervals after it is switched off. Plot a graph of the water's temperature against time.

2 Fill a teapot with boiling water and investigate how its temperature drops with time. Now repeat the experiment when the teapot is wearing a teacosy. Plot the results of both experiments on the same graph. For how long will the tea remain drinkable to you?

3 How does the loss of heat vary for different containers? Compare, for example, coffee mugs, cups, and plastic containers used in automatic drink dispensers. Are some shapes/materials better for retaining heat than others? Investigate.

4 How good is a thermos flask at retaining heat? Start with a thermos of boiling water and measure its temperature at half-hourly intervals.

5 Try to find an algebraic relationship which fits the graphs obtained in your experiments.

References

Look up Newton's law of cooling in a physics textbook.

67 ▪ Cycle design

The wheel has been used for thousands of years – on Roman chariots, 'Wild West' wagons and other forms of transport. The invention of the bicycle is however surprisingly recent. Even steam trains were in use before the first bicycle was created.

Drais, a German forester, made the first machine which looked anything like a bicycle in 1817. It had two wooden wheels joined by a wooden frame and the rider propelled it by pushing backwards against the ground with his feet. This 'running machine' could be steered but had no brakes! Nevertheless Drais was able to travel further and faster on his machine than he could possibly manage on foot.

The development of bicycle design and an analysis of the mechanical/structural advantages of different designs gives a range of project possibilities for all ability levels.

Drais' 'running machine'

1 Historical development

(a) Find out about the velocipede built by the Michaux family for the 1867 Paris exhibition. This was the first cycle to have pedals. How far would it travel forward for one revolution of the pedals?

(b) To improve the gear ratio, cycles were designed with larger driving wheels, the ultimate being the 'penny-farthing'. What is the limitation to the size of the driving wheel of such a design? (See *EMMA*, activity 75, for a detailed discussion of cycle gears.)

(c) The next major improvement was Starley's Rover Safety bicycle in 1885 which had a tubular steel frame and pedals with a chain drive to the rear wheel. Why did this do away with the need of a large driving wheel?

(d) The pneumatic tyre was invented in 1888 by Dunlop. What is the recommended air pressure in a modern cycle tyre and how is it related to the area of the tyre in contact with the ground?

(e) How do the wheels of a modern cycle keep their shape? Contrast the modern design with that of the early cycles with wooden spokes based on wagon wheels.

2 Modern frame design

Look at your friends' cycles and visit a local cycle shop and make a note of all the designs you can find, noting the shape of the frame and wheel sizes.

The design of the frame of the modern girls' cycle shown here is particularly strong as it is made of steel tubes forming interlocking triangles. Make models of this frame and of a modern boys' cycle using card strips and paper fasteners. Which do you think is the better design and why?

Hold AB and see which parts of the frame can move.

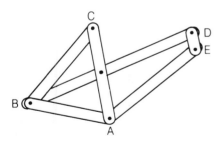

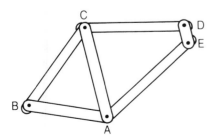

3 Frame sizes

When a racing cyclist wants a new cycle frame he or she orders it by giving the length of the tube AC and the angles C and D of the quadrilateral ACDE. The angle at C, called the seat angle, and the angle at D, called the head angle, can vary by several degrees but are often 72° and 108° giving what is known as a parallel frame. The advantage to the manufacturer is that the lengths of tubes CD and AE can be kept the same and the frame changed only by varying the lengths of AC and DE. Typically AC = 21 in (53 cm) or 23 in (58 cm) but it can be as long as 26 in (66 cm) for a tall rider.

Measure the sizes of the frames of your friends' cycles and find out what sizes your local dealer normally stocks. If there is a local cycling club see what frames they use.

How heavy is a modern bicycle?

4 Cycle gears

The gearing of a bicycle is all important and relates to the distance a cycle moves forward for one revolution of the pedals. How are different gears achieved on a typical 10-gear bicycle?

What gear ratios are possible with hub gears and how can they be compared to derailleur type gears? (See *EMMA*, activity 75.)

How does a hub gear work? Compare the gear ratios of different kinds of bicycles.

References

Cycle brochures
Museums
B. Bolt, *Even More Mathematical Activities* (Cambridge University Press)
S. Strandh, *Machines, An Illustrated History* (Nordbok)
K. Shooter and J. Saxton, *Making Things Work: An Introduction to Design Technology* (Cambridge University Press)

68 · Cranes

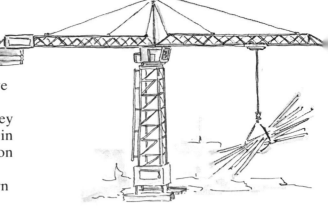

Wherever and whenever heavy objects have to be lifted and moved from one place to another cranes can be seen in operation. They can be seen on building sites, on docksides, in ship-building yards, on the backs of lorries, on oil rigs or on floating barges. How do they work? What are the principles which govern their operation?

1 Tower cranes

One type of crane which catches the eye is the tower crane erected on a building site to rapidly haul skips of concrete and other materials to where they are needed. Such cranes have horizontal jibs (booms) which are built as rigid lightweight steel triangulated structures which can rotate (slew) about a vertical axis on top of a tall tower. They always look very precarious and are delicately balanced with a counterweight on the jib opposite the load to be carried and heavy weights at the base of the tower. Examine any tower cranes you see and note carefully the way in which the tower and jib are constructed. Show that the crane operator can move the crane's hook in three basic ways and hence to anywhere inside a large cylinder. What three coordinates would most conveniently give the hook's position? What is the maximum load such a crane can handle and what is it governed by?

2 Gantry cranes

Gantry cranes are to be found in places like steel works at heavy engineering workshops where a bridge runs up and down the work area on parallel rails carrying on itself a travelling hoist. Investigate their use and how they work.

3 Crane jibs

Dockside cranes and many others have sloping jibs (derricks) and the safe load they can carry depends on the angle of the jib. The radius of the circle on which the hook can rotate also depends on the angle of the jib. How? To move a load towards or away from the centre of its turning circle such a crane has to raise or lower its jib in a process called luffing.

4 Stabilisng mobile cranes

Many cranes are highly mobile and crane hire firms such as Sparrows make their livelihood by being able to drive their cranes along roads and byways to where they are wanted. Before operating such cranes the operator has to extend the outriggers/stabilisers. What is the purpose of these?

5 Pulley systems

Most cranes traditionally had their hook attached to a pulley block and the wire ropes around the pulleys were wound in and out by a winching drum. Show how pulley systems are used to enable large weights to be lifted. What is the (a) velocity ratio, (b) mechanical advantage, (c) efficiency of a pulley system?

Make models of pulley systems to investigate their efficiency.

6 Hydraulic systems

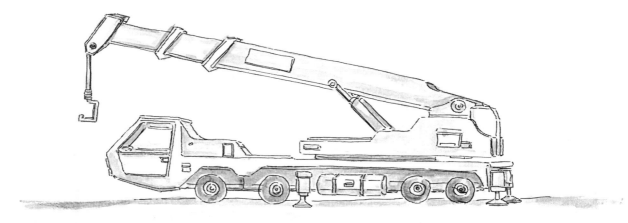

(a) One modern version of the mobile crane has broken away from traditional technology and relies on a telescopic jib and hydraulic rams to change the angle of the jib to the load to where it is required. How does the angle of the jib vary with the length of the hydraulic ram? How can a vertical lift be achieved? What pressure differential is achieved in the hydraulic ram and what force must it exert to lift a 20 tonne load?

(b) Investigate the Hyab hydraulic arms which are permanently carried by some lorries.

7 Specialist cranes

Investigate: floating cranes; railway breakdown cranes; cranes on garage breakdown lorries; cranes for handling freight containers or any other specialist cranes.

8 Model construction

Use construction kits such as Meccano or Fischertechnik to make models of different types of crane and investigate their stability and range of operation.

References

Crane hire firms
Engineering magazines
How Things Work, Vol. 1 (Paladin)
Schools Council Modular Courses in Technology: *Mechanisms* (Oliver and Boyd)
Life Science Library: *Machines* (Time Life)
S. Strandh, *Machines, An Illustrated History* (Nordbok)
K. Shooter and J. Saxton, *Making Things Work: An Introduction to Design Technology* (Cambridge University Press)

69 ▪ Rollers and rolling

Rollers have been used for moving heavy objects from the Egyptians building the pyramids to modern steel mills for moving metal ingots. The properties of rollers and curves of constant breadth make an interesting study.

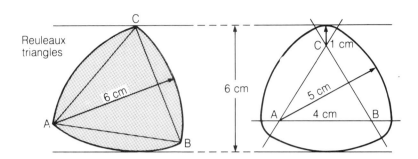

Reuleaux triangles

1 Cylindrical rollers and wheels

(a) How far forward does an object move compared to a roller or wheel which is supporting it?

(b) The point of contact of a rolling object with the ground acts as an instantaneous centre of rotation. Show how, from this, the direction of motion of each point of a rolling object can be determined at any time.

(c) What is the locus of the centre of a 2p coin rolling around the outside of another 2p coin? How many revolutions does the rolling coin make in one circuit?

(d) A circular roller rolls inside a cylinder of twice its diameter. Make a model to show that each point on the circumference of the roller traces out a straight line. (See *MMA*, activity 25.)

(e) Find examples of rollers in use such as for moving baggage at airports.

(f) See what you can find out about cycloids.

2 Curves of constant breadth

There are an infinite number of different shapes which could be used for the cross-section of a roller other than circles, such as the shape of the 50p and 20p coins and Reuleaux triangles (see above), which are known as curves of constant breadth.

Find out how to construct curves of constant breadth based on

(a) regular polygons with an odd number of sides,

(b) star polygons,

(c) any set of intersecting lines.

Show that their perimeter is always πD, where D is their breadth.

Where are curves of constant breadth used?

References

B. Bolt, *Mathematical Activities*, and *More Mathematical Activities (MMA)* (Cambridge University Press)

E. R. Northrop, *Riddles in Mathematics* (Penguin)

M. Gardner, *Further Mathematical Diversions* (Penguin)

70 ▪ Transmitting rotary motion

We are surrounded by mechanisms which involve rotating parts. The modern home may contain, for example, clocks, a food mixer, a washing machine, a vacuum cleaner, a lawn mower, a cassette player, a power drill, a hair dryer, an egg whisk, cycles, a sewing machine, a fishing reel, a car. How is the motor or other input linked to the output? A study of pulleys and belts, of chains and sprockets or of gear trains is highly mathematical and provides a rich source for projects which can give insight into the world in which we live.

1 Pulleys and belts

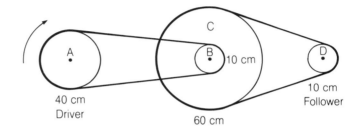

A 40 cm Driver
B 10 cm
C
D 10 cm Follower
60 cm

Pulleys and belts are widely used for linking two rotating shafts. The woollen mills and machine shops since the days of the industrial revolution have used them extensively for transmitting power from the engine to the machines. Look at an electric sewing machine, lawn mower, carpet sweeper or inside a washing machine or at a car engine to see them still in use.

(a) In the pulley system above the diameters of the pulleys are given and shaft A is driven by a motor.

How many turns does shaft B make when A makes one clockwise turn?

How many turns does shaft D make when pulley C makes one clockwise turn?

What happens to shaft D when A makes one clockwise turn?

How can the speed of the following shaft be made (i) smaller, (ii) in the opposite direction to that of the driving shaft?

(b) Find as many examples as you can of belt drive and determine the gear ratio/

velocity ratio/transmission factor used.

How are stepped cone pulleys used (for example, on lathes) to obtain a range of shaft speeds?

(c) Find out the principle behind the Variomatic transmission used in Volvo cars to obtain a variable velocity ratio and do away with a gear box.

See what you can find out about the automatic transmission now available for Ford Fiesta cars.

(d) What is the advantage of a vee belt? When flat belts are used they are often joined in the form of a Möbius strip. Why? In some situations toothed belts and pulleys are used. Why?

When a pulley of radius R drives a pulley of radius r and the centres of the pulleys are a distance d apart, what length belt is required?

(e) Show how pulleys and belts can be used to represent the product of directed numbers.

2 Chains and sprockets

Chains and sprockets are similar to belts and pulleys but here the number of teeth on the sprockets rather than the diameters of the pulleys are the key. Cycles and motorcycles are the commonest applications with derailleur gears an obvious topic.

3 Gear wheels

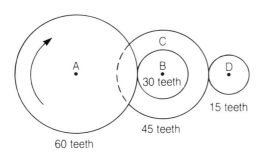

60 teeth
45 teeth
15 teeth

(a) How is the speed of shaft D related to that of shaft A?

(b) Gear wheels come in many shapes and sizes. The gear train shown represents *spur gears* and these are used to transmit motion between parallel shafts. Traditional clocks and watches are full of such gear trains. Investigate a clock mechanism to see how the correct gear ratios are obtained.

(c) Find out about the way in which a car gear box works and, if possible, make a model gear box using a construction kit.

(d) By looking at an egg whisk or a hand drill see how gears can be designed to turn rotation through a right angle. What are *bevel* gears, *contrate* gears and *worm* gears and where, how and why are they used?

(e) See what you can find out about the shape of gear teeth.

4 Miscellaneous

(a) What is a universal coupling and what is its purpose?

(b) Explain the purpose and operation of a clutch.

References

Schools Council, Modular Courses in Technology: *Mechanisms* (Oliver and Boyd)

Schools Council, Mathematics for the Majority Project, *Machines, Mechanisms and Mathematics* by B. Bolt and J. Hiscocks (Chatto and Windus)

D. Lent, Analysis and Design of Mechanisms (Prentice Hall)

How Things Work, Vols. 1 and 2 (Paladin)

B. Bolt, *Even More Mathematical Activities* (Cambridge University Press)

K. Shooter and J. Saxton, *Making Things Work: An Introduction to Design Technology* (Cambridge University Press)

Meccano, Lego Technic, Fischertechnik, etc. include useful parts for experimentation

71 ■ Triangles with muscle

Construction sites abound with mechanical monsters like the JCB excavator shown here which digs trenches or builds embankments with ease. The technology used here based on hydraulic rams is also used in robotics and occurs in modern planes to operate the elevators on the flying surfaces.

How do hydraulic rams work? How are they used?

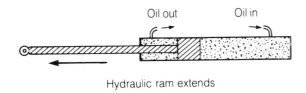

Oil out   Oil in

Hydraulic ram extends

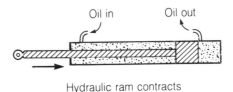

Oil in   Oil out

Hydraulic ram contracts

A hydraulic ram is simply a piston inside a cylinder which is filled with oil. The oil can be pumped under pressure from one side of the piston to the other. This moves the piston along the cylinder, so that the rod to which it is attached moves in or out of the cylinder to change the length of the ram.

1 The force available

How does the force in the piston depend on the area of cross-section of the piston and the difference in pressure on each side of the piston? What kind of pumps are used to give the pressure differential and how large is it?

2 Using the ram for rotation

The hydraulic ram is often used to form one side of a triangular linkage rather like the biceps muscle links the fore arm and upper arm. But the ram has the distinct advantage that it can push as well as pull. Its use is to alter the angle θ between the two rigid arms of the triangle, and what needs investigation is the relationship between the angle θ and the length of AC for different length struts AB and BC.

Make models using card strips or geostrips for AB and BC and a piece of elastic for AC.

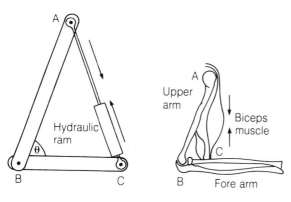

If AC is a hydraulic ram whose length can vary from 1.5 m to 2 m, what lengths should be given to AB and BC to achieve the greatest range of angles for θ?

If the smallest angle θ which can be obtained by such a ram is 30°, what are the lengths of AB and BC? What will be the largest angle obtainable?

3 Practical applications

Study the use of hydraulic rams on tractors, cranes, diggers wherever you find them. Note the relative lengths of AB and BC and the likely maximum and minimum lengths of AC (why must max. AC < 2 × min. AC?). From this work out the range of angles for θ and hence the range of configurations the equipment to which it is attached can take.

4 Models

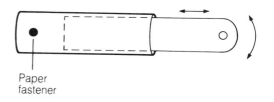

Paper fastener

Make card models to illustrate the variable triangle mechanism, and its use in excavator arms.

The ram can be made as shown here.

If available, experiment by making models with the pneumatic kits now made by Lego and by Fischertechnik. Note that hydraulic rams are pushed by a special hydraulic fluid which does not compress easily, unlike the air in pneumatic models.

5 Further applications

How is the brake pedal in a car linked to the brakes or the clutch pedal to the clutch?

How does hydraulic suspension work and how are on-board computers going to be used in cars to make cars lean inwards when they take a bend?

References

B. Bolt, *More Mathematical Activities*, and *Even More Mathematical Activities* (Cambridge University Press)

How Things Work, Vols. 1 and 2 (Paladin)

Engineering contractors and manufacturers of engineering equipment; see *Yellow Pages* or ask at a local library information centre

72 ▪ Paper sizes and envelopes

An examination of some envelopes show that they come in a variety of sizes and shapes. This is surprising since most sheets of paper are standard sizes. There is opportunity here to find out about paper sizes and to be involved in a simple design problem.

1 Paper sizes

There are internationally agreed sizes of paper designated A0, A1, . . ., A7 with the property that A1 is half an A0 sheet, A2 is half of an A1 sheet, etc. Why is this a useful property?

Abler pupils could show that a consequence is that, for each size, the length of the longer side is $\sqrt{2} \times$ the length of the shorter side, and given that A0 has an area of 1 square metre, the dimensions of all the paper sizes can be determined.

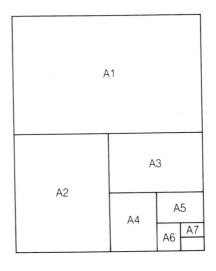

2 Envelope sizes

A4 and A5 are commonly used paper sizes. Design envelopes to contain these sheets. For A4 paper one envelope could be designed to take the sheet when folded into three, and another for when it is folded into four.

Which shapes of envelope do you find most pleasing?

How could the envelopes be cut economically from A0 sheets?

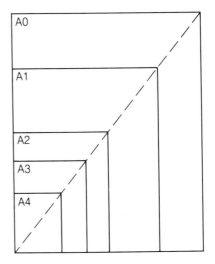

References

SMP, *Book E* (Cambridge University Press)
The Spode Group, *Solving Real Problems with CSE Mathematics* (Cranfield Press)

73 • Measuring inaccessible objects

The word *geometry* originally meant earth measurement. The Egyptians, for example, were very much concerned with surveying – for building pyramids and for reconstructing field boundaries after Nile floods. There are various practical problems which can remind us of the origins of geometry and for which measurement devices can be constructed.

1 Measuring the height of trees

According to the *Guinness Book of Records* the tallest tree in the world has a height of about 112 metres. How can the height of a tree, or of any inaccessible object such as a factory chimney or a church tower, be measured?

(a) One simple method is to use a right-angled isosceles triangle cut from thick card or hardboard. Then, when the top of the tree is sighted along the hypotenuse, the height of the tree above eye level is equal to the distance of the observer from the tree.

   Alternatively, a simple *clinometer* can be made to record the angle of elevation.

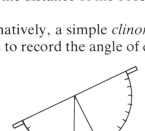

Then, knowing the distance of the observer from the tree, the height can be found by scale drawing or use of trigonometrical functions. Instead of marking the angle on the clinometer it can be graduated in multiplying factors. For example, an angle of elevation of 60° would be marked 1.73, meaning that the distance of the observer from the foot of the tree would need to be multiplied by 1.73.

(b) How can the height be found if the base of the tree is inaccessible?

2 Measuring distances

(a) How can the width of a river be determined without crossing it? Simple methods based on isosceles triangles or enlargement ideas (i.e. elementary trigonometry) can be devised. A horizontal version of a clinometer could be made.

(b) How can the distance of an inaccessible object, such as a tree on the other side of a river, be determined?

References

Schools Council, Mathematics for the Majority Project, *Mathematics from Outdoors* (Chatto and Windus)

74 ■ Surveying ancient monuments

One of the first skills an archaeologist has to learn is the ability to make an accurate survey of the main features of an area. Making a survey of a local castle or hill fort or group of standing stones makes a good subject for a project as well as giving insight and creating interest in local history.

The survey undertaken will depend on what is available to survey in the locality, as well as the sophistication of the equipment available. The minimum requirement is a long tape (say 50 m) but some means for measuring horizontal angles would be helpful. The availability of a theodolite would be a bonus but most schools can probably lay their hands on a prismatic compass. Failing that, two lines drawn using a sighting ruler (alidade) on a drawing board held horizontally and a protractor can be quite satisfactory. Most surveys can be done by triangulating an area and then measuring some offsets to fill in details. The following suggested subjects give an idea of what to look for. In no way is the list exhaustive.

1 In various parts of the country there are stone rows and stone circles from the same period as Stonehenge which would make interesting topics. There are several on Dartmoor and in Cornwall, for example at Merrivale and the Hurlers near Minions. The stone circles at Avebury and the stone circle known as Castlerigg near Keswick are also impressive, while there are many examples in the Peak District.

2 Ancient settlements such as Carn Euny and Chysauster on the Land's End peninsula have a fascination of their own and make good subjects to survey.

3 Ancient enclosures and field systems are further suitable subjects. Grimspound on Dartmoor with all its hut circles is a classic example.

4 Castles abound in some areas whether of the stone variety such as Caernarvon or hill forts which are little more than earth mounds from a much earlier period, such as Badbury Rings in Dorset, or Mam Tor in the Peak District.

References

B. Bolt, *Even More Mathematical Activities*, activity 19 (Cambridge University Press)

J. E. Wood, *Sun, Moon and Standing Stones* (Oxford University Press)

T. Clare, *Archaeological Sites of Devon and Cornwall* (Moorland Publishing)

Peak District National Park (HMSO)

Some references which include surveying are:

Schools Council, *Mathematics from Outdoors* (Chatto and Windus)

SMP, *Book 1* (Cambridge University Press)

E. Williams and H. Shuard, *Primary Mathematics Today* (Longman)

75 · Paper folding

Paper folding is a much neglected activity as far as geometry is concerned. It can give very clear demonstrations of many basic properties, provide nets for solids and give insights to symmetry, making it an ideal topic for a project.

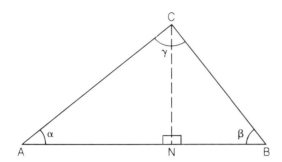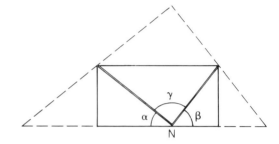

1 Properties of triangles

(a) The angle sum of a triangle can be neatly demonstrated. Cut out a triangle ABC. Fold through C so that B comes onto AB to give the altitude CN. Fold each corner of the triangle so that the vertices A, B and C meet at N. Clearly $\alpha + \beta + \gamma = 180°$.

(b) Cut out four more triangles, preferably acute angled, and produce fold lines to show that:
  (i) the angle bisectors are concurrent;
  (ii) the altitudes are concurrent;
  (iii) the medians are concurrent;
  (iv) the perpendicular bisectors are concurrent.

(c) In the centre of a large sheet of paper draw a triangle ABC. Now make folds which bisect the interior and exterior angles of triangle ABC. Their intersection gives the centre of the incircle. Similarly the bisectors of the exterior angles of the triangle give the centres of the three escribed circles.

2 Folding polygons

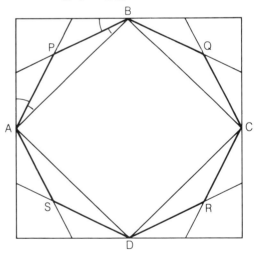

(a) Show how to fold a pair of parallel lines and a rectangle. From the rectangle it is not now difficult to fold a square. The adjoining diagram shows how to obtain a regular octagon. A, B, C, D are the mid-points of the large square. P, Q, R and S are found by folding the angle bisectors AP, BP, etc.

(b) Show how to fold a parallelogram, a rhombus, a kite, an arrow and an isosceles triangle.

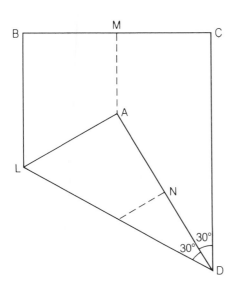

(c) Show how to fold an equilateral triangle. This depends on a method for folding an angle of 60° and is surprisingly easy. Fold a rectangle ABCD in half along MN. Now fold corner A through D so that A lies on MN. Angle ADL is then equal to 30°, so angle LDC is 60°. It is not difficult from this to fold an equilateral triangle and then to obtain a regular hexagon. Can you prove that angle LDA = 30°? (See *EMMA*, activity 18.)

(d) It is also possible to fold a regular pentagon. This depends on the fact that the ratio of the diagonal of a regular pentagon to its side is the golden section ratio ½(√5 + 1) and that √5 can be folded as the hypotenuse of a right-angled triangle whose sides are 2 units and 1 unit.

3 Pythagoras' theorem

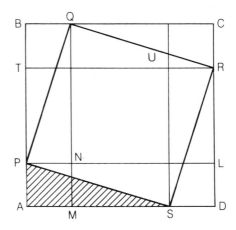

By folding the pattern shown in the diagram a demonstration of Pythagoras' theorem is soon evident. Referring to their areas
square ABCD = square PQRS +
                4 × triangle ASP
but square ABCD is also equal to
  square APNM + square NQCL +
  4 × triangle ASP
but square NQCL = square ASUT
so   square PQRS = square APNM +
                     square ASUT
See also *EMMA*, activity 60.

4 Folding an ellipse

An ellipse can also be produced as an envelope of lines starting with a circle of paper, marking a point inside it and folding the circumference of the circle to just touch the point. See *MA*, activity 15.

References

B. Bolt, *Mathematical Activities (MA)*, and *Even More Mathematical Activities (EMMA)* (Cambridge University Press)

T. Sundara Row, *Geometric Exercises in Paper Folding* (Dover)

R. Harbin, *Origami* (Hodder)

76 ▪ Spirals

Spirals are not often studied in the main school syllabus but as a commonly occurring curve the spiral forms a good topic for a project, and deserves to be better understood.

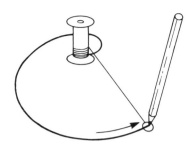

1 Archimedean spirals

(a) Wind a piece of string around a cotton reel. Tie a small loop to the free end of the string. Hold the cotton reel down on a piece of paper, put a pencil in the loop, pull it taut and, keeping it taut, draw a locus on the paper as you unwind the string from the reel.

This locus is known as an Archimedean spiral – Archimedes was the first person to make a detailed study of it. One of the main properties of the curve is that the distance between adjacent coils is always the same and this suggests another way of drawing the curve.

(b) On polar graph paper start at the pole and move out one circle say for each 30° you rotate; the result is another Archimedean spiral. In general, if the radius r is related to the angle θ by the relation $r = k\theta$, where k is constant, a spiral always results.

Experiment with different values of k – positive, fractional, negative, etc. – and see what results. If you have access to a microcomputer, write a program to give the spiral.

(c) The curve occurs in many places, it corresponds to the rolled edge of say a carpet or cassette tape or toilet roll. It approximates to the shape of a coiled snake and corresponds to the groove in a record, or the wound spring in a clock, or in a cane and raffia coiled mat. See what other examples you can find.

(d) Find out how a cam in the shape of an Archimedean spiral is used in mechanisms to change rotary to linear motion.

2 Equiangular spirals

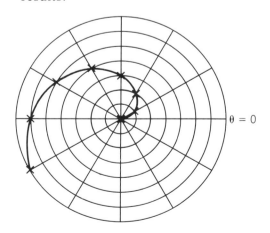

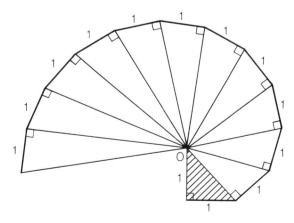

(a) Make a copy of this diagram. Start with the isosceles right-angled triangle (shaded) and build up a sequence of right-angled triangles on the hypotenuse of the previous one as shown. The outer boundary of lines, each of unit length, approximates to the curve known as the equiangular or logarithmic spiral. Its name comes from the property that all radial lines drawn from O will always cut the curve at the same constant angle.

What are the lengths of the radial lines in the diagram?

The famous mathematician Jacob Bernoulli (1654–1705) was so fascinated by the curve that he had it carved on his tombstone.

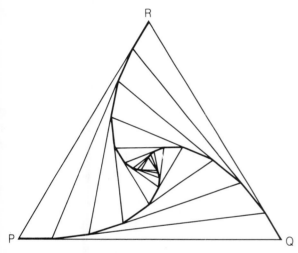

(b) If three dogs start simultaneously at the vertices PQR of an equilateral triangle and run so that P chases Q, Q chases R and R chases P, then their paths will be parts of equiangular spirals. See *MA*, activities 4 and 5.

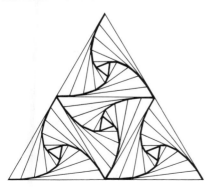

(c) Squares can be constructed to form a sequence of rectangles whose sides are consecutive numbers in the Fibonacci sequence (see *MA*, activity 146) and by drawing quadrants of circles in the squares a very good approximation to an equiangular spiral results. Draw one for yourself.

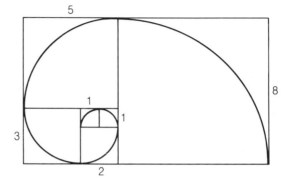

(d) Equiangular spirals occur in nature in many ways: in a spider's web; as the pattern of seeds in a sunflower head; as the flow of water in a whirl pool; as the spiral on a snail shell, or the distribution of stars in galaxies. Try to find pictures of these and of other examples.

References

M. Gardner, *Further Mathematical Diversions* (Penguin)

L. Mottershead, *Sources of Mathematical Discovery* (Basil Blackwell)

E. H. Lockwood, *A Book of Curves* (Cambridge University Press)

Exploring Mathematics on Your Own: Curves (John Murray)

J. Pearcy and K. Lewis, *Experiments in Mathematics, Stage 2* (Longman)

H. Steinhaus, *Mathematical Snapshots* (Oxford University Press)

B. Bolt, *Mathematical Activities (MA)* (Cambridge University Press)

77 ▪ Patchwork patterns

Patchwork patterns are a fascinating subset of two-dimensional tessellations based on fitting together simple polygons of different materials to give dramatic designs. A study of the traditional designs will lead to a good understanding of the nature of a tessellation and repeating patterns.

The starting point for this project is ideally to obtain a book or books on patchwork design. Dover Publications produce a good selection of such books, some of which are likely to be available in the library.

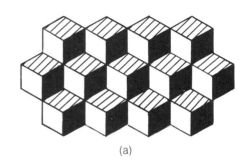

(a)

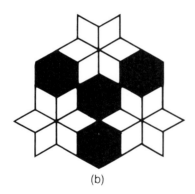

(b)

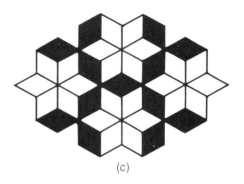

(c)

1 Many designs are based on using a single shape such as a square or regular hexagon. The designs shown above are all based on a rhombus which is itself equivalent to two equilateral triangles. In each design the rhombi fit together in the same way with either six acute angles meeting at a point or three obtuse angles together. The different designs are obtained by the mix of colours used and the way they are distributed.

In (a) three colours are used in equal proportions. In (b) there are two colours in equal proportions while in (c) there are twice as many white as black rhombi.

A good way to get started on this topic is to copy a number of the designs. The use of squared paper or isometric paper helps but it may be more appropriate to start by cutting out a cardboard template of the shape required and drawing around it.

2 In each pattern there is a basic *unit of design* which is the smallest area of the pattern which, if repeated, would produce the whole pattern. The unit is usually composed of several of the individual shapes. The more complex the pattern, the more shapes will be needed in the unit of design. Examples shown here are for the three patterns above. These units are not unique, but any alternative will contain the same number of shapes with the same proportions of colours.

(a)

(b)

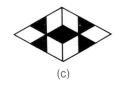

(c)

Picking out other units of design for the same patterns can be very instructive and could be seen as part of such a project.

3 Many traditional patterns are based on squares and half squares which, suitably arranged, produce very attractive designs. In these more than one shape is often used, but starting with squared paper it is not difficult to draw them. See the examples here.

Broken
dishes

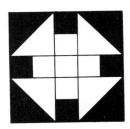

The wrench

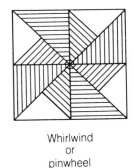

Whirlwind
or
pinwheel

4 In addition to analysing and drawing traditional patterns try to be original. Design new patterns and make them up by sticking coloured shapes onto a plain background. The Cambridge Microsoftware program *Tessellations* is a very powerful tool for creating new patterns on a BBC micro.

5 Links can be made with mosaics, tiling patterns, wallpaper patterns and curtain materials.

References

R. McKim, *101 Patchwork Patterns* (Dover)
C. B. Grafton, *Geometric Patchwork Patterns* (Dover)
B. Bolt, *Even More Mathematical Activities* (Cambridge University Press)
Cambridge Microsoftware: *Tessellations*, by Homerton College (Cambridge University Press)

78 ▪ Space filling

Many shapes are designed so that they pack together to fill space without leaving any gaps in the same way that some shapes in two dimensions form a tessellation. The point of this project is to investigate shapes which can be used to fill space.

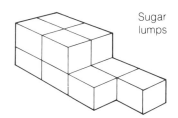

Sugar lumps

1 Packing cubes and cuboids

The simplest shape for filling space is the cube which can be seen packed in boxes of sugar lumps or OXO cubes or children's bricks. Cuboids are even more common as many foods are packaged in cuboid containers. They abound everywhere as builders' bricks and can be seen on farms as straw bales or on modern shipping as large containers.

Triangular prism

(a) Make a note of different examples of cubes and cuboids which you see packed together.

(b) Investigate what size cuboids can and cannot be made by fitting together $2 \times 1 \times 1$ blocks (i.e. cuboid blocks equivalent to two cubes).

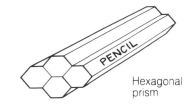

Hexagonal prism

(c) Find the dimensions of the standard bricks and blocks used in building houses and try to explain their relative sizes.

(d) What can you say about the dimensions of a cuboid which when cut in half forms two cuboids of the same shape as the original?

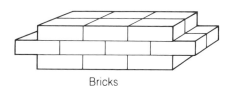

Bricks

(e) A product is first packed in a $2 \times 1 \times 1$ carton and then twelve of these are packed into a $4 \times 3 \times 2$ box. Investigate the different ways the box can be packed.

Trapezium prism

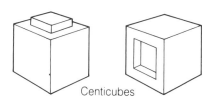

Centicubes

2 Other space-filling shapes

Shapes other than cuboids can be fitted together to fill space.

(a) *Prisms* with a variety of cross-sections are possible and occur for example as hexagonal pencils or giant crystals in the Giants' Causeway.

(b) *Parallelipipeds*, rather like cuboids but with opposite faces identical parallelograms instead of rectangles, also fill space. See what examples of these you can find and make a parallelipiped from card or using drinking straws joined by pipe cleaners.

(c) Cubes can be divided into *pyramids*, or in half, in a variety of ways which clearly produce solids which fill space. See *MA*, activity 79, and *MMA*, activities 2, 3 and 4 for details.

(d) The *rhombic dodecahedron*, whose twelve faces are identical rhombuses, is another fascinating space-filling solid which occurs naturally as the shape of the cell in a beehive. It also occurs naturally as the shape of the mineral garnet. The easiest way to visualise the solid is to start with a cube and then stick pyramids whose heights are half that of the cube on each of its faces. Make a model. What is the volume of this shape related to the cube?

(e) Investigate the *shapes you can make with four identical cubes* and then see which of these are space-filling solids. (NB. Multicubes make a helpful visual aid.)

(f) So far only single shapes have been considered. The next stage is to investigate *pairs of complementary shapes* such as regular octahedrons and regular tetrahedrons which can easily be modelled in a variety of techniques.

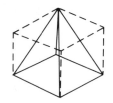

Some pyramids from cubes

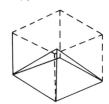

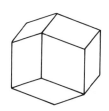

Rhombic dodecahedron

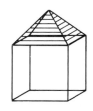

References

B. Bolt, *Mathematical Activities (MA)*, and *More Mathematical Activities (MMA)* (Cambridge University Press)

H. M. Cundy and A. P. Rollett, *Mathematical Models* (Tarquin)

H. Steinhaus, *Mathematical Snapshots* (Oxford University Press)

A. F. Wells, *The Third Dimension in Chemistry* (Oxford University Press)

S. W. Golomb, *Polyominoes* (Allen and Unwin)

SMP, *Book E* (Cambridge University Press)

See Crystals, project 89

79 · Packing

When articles have to be stored or transported it is often desirable to pack them as efficiently as possible so that the proportion of wasted space is made as small as possible. The shape of some objects such as cuboids can be fitted together without leaving any gaps but others such as cylinders and spheres are inevitably inefficient. The basis of this project is to investigate the relative efficiency of packing different shaped objects.

Shapes which fill space without leaving any gaps have been considered in 'Space filling' (project 78) but could also be used in this project.

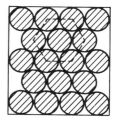

Hexagonal packing

1 Packing cylinders

Many foods and drinks are sold in cylindrical tins which are packed into cuboid boxes for delivery to the retailer. These can be packed in two essentially different ways, known as square packing and hexagonal packing. Use coins to investigate these ways.

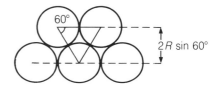

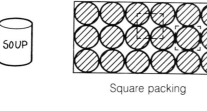

Square packing

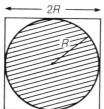

(a) With square packing the efficiency can be measured as the percentage of the box occupied by the tin which is clearly seen as the ratio of a circle to its bounding square and is always

$$\frac{\pi R^2}{(2R)^2} \times 100 \simeq 78.5\%$$

(b) With hexagonal packing the number of tins makes a difference, for although in one sense they are closer together the gaps at the ends of alternate rows are large. With the 18 tins packed as shown it is necessary to compute the dimensions of the box and then consider the ratio of the volume of the 18 tins to the volume of the box. A little consideration will show that the distance between two adjacent rows of tins will be $2R \sin 60°$ and that the cross-section of the box will have dimensions
$$(2R + 8R \sin 60°) \times 8R$$
This leads to a packing efficiency of about 79.2% which is an improvement on the square packing.

(c) What is the most efficient way of packing 50 tins?

(d) Investigate how cylindrical objects are packed such as circular straw bales, drinking straws, pipes, beer cans, toilet rolls.

2 Packing spheres

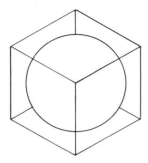

Squash balls are often marketed in individual cubical boxes so that the efficiency of packing is clearly related to the ratio of the ball's volume to the volume of the containing box:

$$\frac{4/3\pi r^3}{(2r)^3} \times 100 \simeq 52\%$$

Tennis balls are often sold in boxes of six in an arrangement which gives the same efficiency, but they are also sold in packs of four in cylindrical tubes. What is the efficiency then?

Spheres can be packed in many ways which are best investigated by experimenting with a large number of equal spheres such as marbles or the polystyrene balls used in chemistry for building molecules. See for example pp. 220–1 in *Mathematical Snapshots* by Steinhaus.

Apples approximate to spheres. How are they packed?

3 Packing other shapes

Investigate the packing of shapes such as light bulbs, milk bottles, hens' eggs, Easter eggs, chocolates, soap, toothpaste tubes, shampoo bottles, biscuits, yoghurt containers.

Most of these objects are packed in cuboid shaped boxes whose volume is easy to obtain, but how can the volume of the object itself be obtained? It may be possible to approximate to the volume by modelling it with two or more shapes whose volume can be found. A light bulb can be seen to approximate to a sphere and a cylinder, for example. However, other shapes are not so easy to come to terms

with by this approach. But the principle of displacement could be used. If the object is submerged in a suitable container of water the change in the water level can be used to determine its volume.

4 Designing furniture

How efficiently are the books packed on the shelves of the library? If you were to design a bookcase with four shelves how would you space the shelves?

Investigate stacking chairs by comparing the room space they occupy when stacked and when in use.

References

H. Steinhaus, *Mathematical Snapshots* (Oxford University Press)

A. F. Wells, *The Third Dimension in Chemistry* (Oxford University Press)

H. M. Cundy and A. P. Rollett, *Mathematical Models* (Tarquin)

M. Gardner, *New Mathematical Diversions* (Penguin)

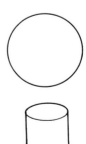

80 ▪ Cones

Cones, and truncated cones, are of frequent occurrence in the world around us. There are various design problems associated with these shapes which can give rise to interesting projects. Also some important curves occur as sections of cones.

1 Cone models

Make cones of different types – tall, thin ones like ice-cream cones; short, wide ones like Chinese hats. What determines the shape of a cone? How much information is needed to make a cone? Construct cones given (a) the semi-vertical angle and the sloping height, (b) the diameter of the base and the vertical height.

2 Truncated cones

Make truncated cones like a yoghurt pot. Experiment with various slopes for the sides. Compare the dimensions of containers for yoghurt, cream, margarine, etc. What information is needed to make such containers? Design a container to hold 150 ml of cream. Generalise your method.

3 Lampshades

Lampshade frames can be bought at handicraft shops in standard sizes. The material – cloth, parchment, etc. – then has to be cut to fit. How would you set about it? Give general instructions for any frame.

4 Conic sections

Cones were studied by the Greeks in about 250 BC. Appollonius of Perga was interested in the different curves which could be obtained by taking sections of a cone. He found essentially three different types of conic section which he called an ellipse, a parabola and a hyperbola. Although he did not realise at the time, these curves all occur in practical situations. Ellipses occur as orbits of planets and satellites. The path of a cricket ball, ignoring air resistance, is a parabola; reflectors for electric fires are parabolic. Hyperbolas can often be seen on walls as shadows of a lampshade.

A simple demonstration of these curves can be carried out using a plastic funnel, or, better, a glass funnel borrowed from the chemistry laboratory, and a bowl of water. By partially immersing the funnel and holding it at various angles, the curves can be seen.

More permanent models to show the sections can be made from thick card.

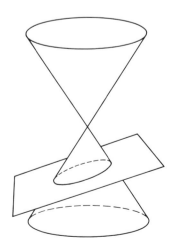

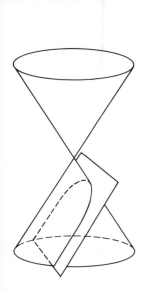 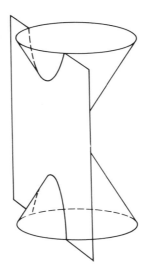

5 Rolling up hill

An amusing model in which a cone appears to roll uphill can be made by taping two plastic funnels together and constructing an incline from card. Appropriate adjustment of the angle of the card might be needed.

6 The shortest distance

Show how to find the shortest distance between two points on the surface of a cone.

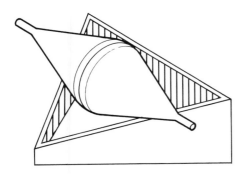

References

H. M. Cundy and A. P. Rollett, *Mathematical Models* (Tarquin)

H. Courant and H. Robbins, *What is Mathematics?* (Oxford University Press)

A. Fishburn, *The Batsford Book of Lampshades* (Batsford)

B. Bolt, *Mathematical Activities*, activities 13–17, 66, 93, and *More Mathematical Activities*, activities 70, 71 (Cambridge University Press)

81 · Three-dimensional representation

It is often necessary to represent three-dimensional objects on paper. Artists began to tackle the problem in the fifteenth century and this led to projective geometry, the mathematical study of perspective. More recently, standard methods for representing buildings and components have been devised for use by architects and engineers. This topic should appeal to pupils doing craft, design and technology.

1 Perspective

(a) Books such as *The Story of Art* and *Mathematics in Western Culture* give examples of the early use of perspective by artists such as Paolo Uccello, Piero della Francesca and Albrecht Dürer. They contain sufficient material to form the basis of a project.
(b) Draw some objects in perspective; for example, a perspective view of a floor made up of square tiles.
(c) What shapes can be obtained as shadows of a square?

2 Isometric drawings

A second commonly-used method for representing three-dimensional objects is on *isometric* paper (an equilateral triangle grid).

A possible project: using interlocking cubes, such as Multilink cubes, find how many ways there are to fit four cubes together. Draw them on isometric paper. (Harder: repeat for five cubes.)

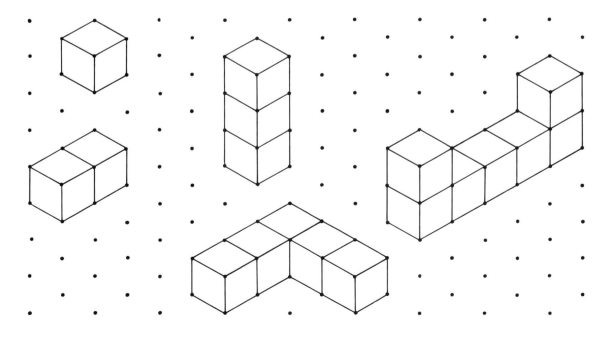

3 Plans and elevations

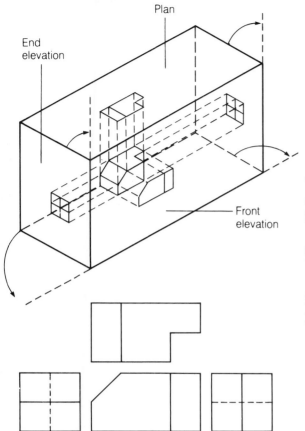

The standard method of plans and elevations used by architects and engineers was invented by the Frenchman Gaspard Monge in 1795. In effect, he imagined the object inside a glass box and drew the projection of the object on the faces of the box. The box was then opened out.

A possible project is to design a building such as a house and draw the plan view and the elevations.

4 Impossible objects

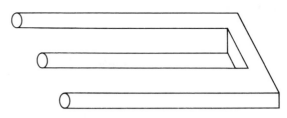

The eye can easily be deceived by two-dimensional pictures. A well-known example is shown here.

The artist M. C. Escher has used the idea in some interesting ways – see *The Graphic Work of M. C. Escher*.

Find some examples of drawings of impossible objects and try to make some yourself.

References

E. Gombrich, *The Story of Art* (Phaidon)

M. Kline, *Mathematics in Western Culture* (Oxford University Press)

SMP, *New Book 5* (Cambridge University Press)

F. Dubery and J. Willats, *Perspective and Other Drawing Systems* (Herbert Press)

L. B. Ballinger, *Perspective, Space and Design* (Van Nostrand, Reinhold)

B. Bolt, *More Mathematical Activities* (Cambridge University Press)

The Graphic Work of M. C. Escher (Pan)

B. Ernst, *Adventures with Impossible Figures* (Tarquin)

SMP 11–16, G *Impossible Objects* (Cambridge University Press)

C. Caket, *An Introduction to Perspective*, and *Getting Things into Perspective* (Macmillan Educational)

82 ▪ Three-dimensional surfaces

Curve-stitching in two dimensions is a popular activity in schools. The corresponding idea in three dimensions is not seen as frequently but it provides some useful opportunities for constructional skills and the results can be very striking.

1 Curved surfaces from straight lines

Curved surfaces made from straight lines sound impossible. But they can be made and some architects have used the idea to construct curved roofs from straight timbers.

A model of such a roof can be made by cutting two triangles of card about 15 cm long and 5 cm high with bases which allow them to stand upright. Drinking straws are then laid across the triangles as shown. Stronger models can be made by using strips of balsa glued together.

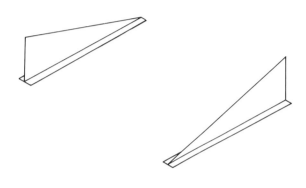

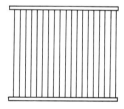

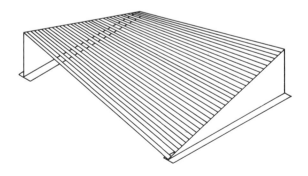

A dynamic model can be made using two pieces of wood (0.5 cm circular dowel is convenient, but any cross-section will do), or strips of Meccano, connected by shirring elastic. If using wood, drill holes at 1 cm intervals. Then, by holding the supports with the elastic under tension, and rotating them, curved surfaces can be made to appear.

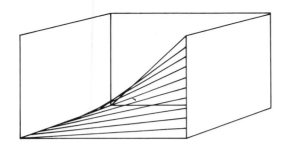

A permanent model can be made in a cardboard box with the front and top removed. An even more interesting model can be made in a tetrahedron.

2 A cooling tower model

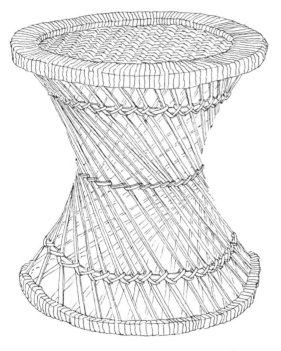

A cooling tower model can be made from two circles of corrugated cardboard about 6 cm in radius with holes at 20° intervals. Drinking straws are then pushed through corresponding holes. When one disc is rotated a curved surface is formed.

A more-permanent model can be made using wooden (or better, perspex) circles held together by dowel or metal rods and connected by shirring elastic. See *MA*, activity 94.

3 A parabolic bowl

Points in three-dimensional space can be defined by three coordinates (x, y, z). Surfaces can then be described by relationships between the coordinates. For example, $z = x^2 + y^2$ is the equation of a parabolic bowl. Vertical sections are parabolas and horizontal sections are circles. A model can be made from card by cutting appropriate parabolas (using a template drawn on graph paper) and circles which are then slotted so that they fit together.

References

H. M. Cundy and A. P. Rollett. *Mathematical Models* (Tarquin)

B. Bolt, *Mathematical Activities (MA)* (Cambridge University Press)

H. Steinhaus, *Mathematical Snapshots* (Oxford University Press)

83 ▪ Curves from straight lines

The idea of an envelope curve formed from straight lines (or from curves) is a familiar one in mathematics. In recent years it has become popular as an art form with kits available in handicraft shops.

1 Curves from straight lines

(a) Mark ten points, say, at 1 cm intervals on two lines at right angles, numbering them 1 to 10. Join 1 to 10, 2 to 9 etc. The result is a parabola.

   Experiment with the lines at other angles.

   Use the adjacent sides of polygons. Make some 'pictures' using the idea.

(b) Instead of drawing the lines, stitch them by making holes and joining the points using needle and thread. White thread on black card is attractive.

(c) Design and make a nail-and-thread kit, including instructions.

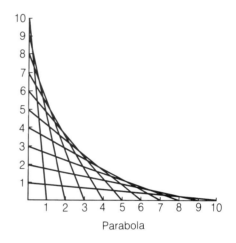

Parabola

2 Joining points on a circle

(a) Draw a circle and mark it at 10° intervals using a circular protractor. Number the points from 0 to 35. Using a 'multiply by 3' rule join 1 to 3, 2 to 6, 3 to 9, etc. The result is a curve called a nephroid (meaning kidney shape). The curve, or rather half of it, can sometimes be seen on the surface of a cup of tea or coffee. It is caused by reflection of rays of light in the side of the cup.

(b) Try other rules. For example, 'multiply by 2' gives a cardioid. See *MMA*, activity 69.

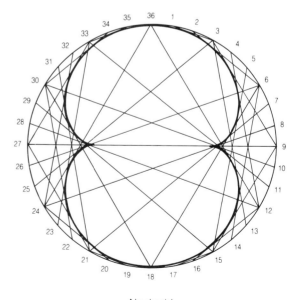

Nephroid

3 Making shapes with circles

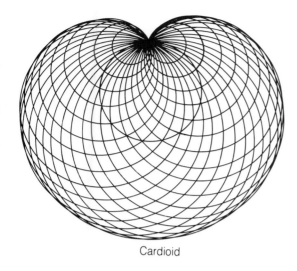

Cardioid

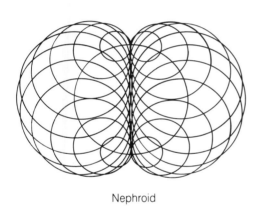

Nephroid

4 Computer programs

Computer programs can be written to produce these curves. For example, this program draws a parabola:

```
10 MODE 1
20 FOR X = 0 TO 900 STEP 50
30 MOVE X,0
40 DRAW 0,900−X
50 FOR I = 0 TO 200 : NEXT I
60 NEXT X
```

The nephroid can be drawn with the following program:

```
10 MODE 1
20 T = PI/18
30 FOR I = 1 TO 35
40 MOVE 600 + 400 * SIN (I*T),
      500 + 400 * COS (I*T)
50 DRAW 600 + 400 * SIN (3*I*T),
      500 + 400 * COS (3*I*T)
60 FOR J = 1 TO 200 : NEXT J
70 NEXT I
```

See also *132 Short Programs for the Mathematics Classroom* for the parabola and variations on it.

5 Extensions

Ellipses and parabolas can be formed in a variety of ways from straight lines. See *MA*, activity 15, and *MMA*, activities 70 and 71.

(a) A cardioid can also be obtained as the envelope of circles whose centres are all on a fixed circle and which pass through a fixed point on that circle.
(b) A nephroid is the envelope of circles whose centres are on a given circle and which are all tangential to a diameter of that circle.

References

E. H. Lockwood, *A Book of Curves* (Cambridge University Press)

Mathematical Association, *132 Short Programs for the Mathematics Classroom* (Stanley Thornes)

B. Bolt, *Mathematical Activities (MA)*, and *More Mathematical Activities (MMA)* (Cambridge University Press)

Leapfrogs, *Curves* (Tarquin)

J. Holding, *Mathematical Roses* (Cambridge Microsoftware: Cambridge University Press)

84 ▪ Mathematics in biology

In mathematics lessons, enlargement, Fibonacci sequences and probability are often dealt with in isolation. These ideas arise naturally in biology and can be explored through various projects.

1 Sizes of animals

Why do giants not exist? Why do rats not grow as big as elephants? How does an animal like a rabbit keep warm in winter? Why is it dangerous for a fly to get wet? Why do the largest animals, whales, live in the sea?

The key idea behind these questions is that of enlargement: when an object is enlarged by a linear factor of 3, its area is multiplied by 9 and its volume by 27. An animal's heat control system depends on its surface area, the strength of bones depends on their cross-sectional area, weight depends on volume, work done in moving depends on volume of muscle, etc.

2 Fibonacci sequences

(a) Fibonacci is said to have arrived at his sequence by consideration of a model of the breeding of rabbits. He assumed that a pair of rabbits produces another pair every month beginning when they are two months old. Show that, starting with one pair, the number of pairs in successive months is

1, 1, 2, 3, 5, 8, . . .

(b) A male bee (a drone) is produced by the unfertilised egg of a queen, but a queen is produced by a fertilised egg. The number of bees in the family tree of a drone follows the Fibonacci sequence.

The diagram shows the family tree going back to the 'great-grandparents' of a drone. It can be continued backwards to show previous generations.

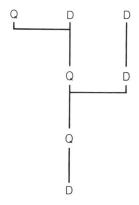

(c) The shoots or leaves on a stem occur at different angles. On hawthorn, apple and oak, a spiral around a stem making 2 complete turns passes through 5 shoots. For poplar and pear, a spiral of 3 turns passes through 8 shoots. For willow, a spiral of 5 turns passes through 8 shoots. Examine shoots from various trees in this way.

(d) The scales of a fir-cone or a pineapple are arranged in five rows sloping up to the right and eight to the left. Heads of daisies and sunflowers often have 21 spirals of florets growing in one direction and 34 in the other. Obtain some fir-cones, etc. and check the occurrence of Fibonacci numbers.

3 Models in genetics

When plants or animals reproduce, the characteristics of the offspring are determined by the random combination of different types of genes. The foundations of genetics were laid by Mendel (1865) who carried out experiments on hybrid peas.

A simple model involves two types of gene which give rise to three genotypes in the offspring. A simulation can be carried out using one sampling bottle for the males and one for the females, each containing coloured beads in the ratio of the genes. The nature of the offspring is determined by picking one bead from the male bottle and one from the female bottle.

References

J. B. S. Haldane, *On Being the Right Size* (Oxford University Press)

D'Arcy Thompson, *On Growth and Form* (Cambridge University Press)

R. F. Gibbons and B. A. Blofield, *Life Size* (Macmillan) (out of print)

F. W. Land, *The Language of Mathematics* (Murray)

P. S. Stevens, *Patterns in Nature* (Penguin)

E. R. Northrop, *Riddles in Mathematics* (Penguin)

J. Ling, *Mathematics across the Curriculum* (Blackie)

J. Lighthill (ed.), *Newer Uses of Mathematics* (Penguin)

85 ▪ Making maps

There is a problem in making a map of the earth because it is not possible to represent a spherical surface on a flat piece of paper without distortion. As a study of an atlas shows, various solutions have been arrived at, depending on what is to be preserved – distance, area, angle, etc. There is scope here for a project finding out the properties of the various methods used and possibly making models to illustrate the principles.

1 Gnomonic projection

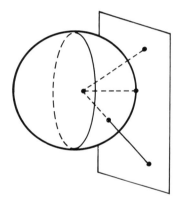

In this method the surface of the earth is projected from the centre onto a tangent plane. Great circles project onto straight lines. This has the advantage that the shortest distance routes for ships and planes appear as straight lines on the map. A disadvantage is that points near the edge of the hemisphere appear too far out on the map with consequent distortion of distances, angles and areas.

2 Stereographic projection

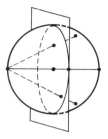

The sphere is projected from a point on the surface onto a plane through the centre as shown. In this method angles are preserved but area is not. The region in the centre is about one quarter of its actual size on the globe.

3 Cylindrical projection

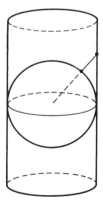

(a) The sphere is projected from the centre onto a cylinder surrounding it, which is then cut along a vertical line and opened out. The lines of latitude appear as horizontals and the lines of longitude as verticals. Problems arise near the poles. The true distance at latitude α is the distance on the map multiplied by $\cos \alpha$.

(b) Mercator's projection is a cylindrical projection in which a vertical distortion factor is chosen equal to the horizontal factor, $\cos \alpha$. The area factor is then $(\cos \alpha)^2$. The consequent distortion can be seen in that Greenland appears to be about the same size as South America although it is only about one ninth as large.

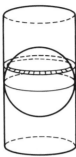

(c) Another method of cylindrical projection is to project circles of latitude from their centres onto the cylinder. Similarly for the circles of longitude. This projection has the property that area is conserved. Archimedes was familiar with this property (an implication is that the area of a sphere is the same as the area of its circumscribing cylinder).

　　Examples of map projections are given in *The Arnold World Atlas*.

4 Some other types of map

(a) Maps showing rail and air line routes are often simplified. The map of the London underground is a well-known example. What features do such maps show? Obtain some examples. Make a map of this type relating to the locality.

(b) When travelling by rail it is the time taken to reach the destination which is of importance rather than the distance. Maps can be drawn in which lengths represent the time taken to travel by train from London, say. It is usual to show the places on their correct bearing. By obtaining the latest national timetable a 'time map' could be drawn showing the positions of major cities. A map could be drawn to show the time taken by children to get to school from various places in the locality.

(c) Some atlases contain maps in which countries are drawn with their areas representing a particular property. (See for example *The Times Concise Atlas of the World* and *The New State of the World Atlas*.)

References

M. Kline, *Mathematics in Western Culture* (Penguin)

H. Steinhaus, *Mathematical Snapshots* (Oxford University Press)

SMP, *New Book 4 Part 2* (Cambridge University Press)

The Arnold World Atlas (Arnold)

The Times Concise Atlas of the World

The New State of the World Atlas (Heinemann)

K. Selkirk, *Pattern and Place* (Cambridge University Press)

SMP 11–16, *Book Y5* (Cambridge University Press)

86 ▪ Mathematics in geography

In recent years school geography has become more quantitative. There are some aspects of the subject which could provide opportunities for cooperative work on projects.

1 Compactness

Geographers are often interested in the way in which villages and towns have developed. Some settlements might be roughly circular; some might straggle along a road or valley; others might be star-shaped where they have grown along main roads. The provision of bus services, refuse collections, schools, sports facilities, etc. can depend on the shape of the settlement. It might be helpful therefore to quantify shape.

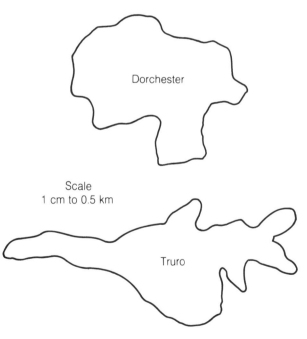

Dorchester

Scale
1 cm to 0.5 km

Truro

Devise some methods for quantifying the compactness of a shape. (Possible methods might involve comparison with circles.)

2 The best site

(a) Where is the best place for a radio transmitter to cover the whole of England and Wales?

Where should it be sited if it is to cover the most land possible but not the sea?

Suppose four transmitters with ranges of 200 km are to be sited. Where would you put them?

Are there places which are not adequately covered at the moment by radio and television transmitters? Make suggestions for improvement.

(b) Suppose a large hospital is to be built serving three towns. Where should it be built? Its site will need to take account of the distribution of the population in the three towns.

One way to find the minimising position is to put a large map of the region on a board and make holes at the positions of the towns. Then tie three strings together, put the ends through the holes and fix weights to them proportional to the populations. The knot will give the required position.

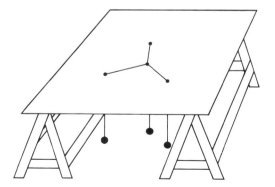

Investigate a siting problem of this type in your own locality.

3 Designing road systems

Three towns, A, B and C are to be connected by roads. It is required to make the total length of the roads as short as possible. How can it be done?

The surprising result is that the required point P is such that the angles between AP, BP and CP are all 120°. (When one of the angles of the triangle, C say, is greater than 120° then P is at C.)

The problem can be modelled using soap solution! Soap film has the property that it takes up the minimum area. If a soap film is formed between two sheets of perspex about 3 cm apart connected by three pins representing the three towns it will give the minimum road system.

The result for four towns is even more surprising.

It is recommended that a good quality washing-up liquid is used to make the soap solution.

It is also interesting from the mathematical aspect to investigate the surfaces formed when skeleton polyhedra made of wire are dipped into the soap solution.

4 Colouring maps

What is the smallest number of colours needed to colour a map so that adjacent countries are coloured differently?

This is a famous problem. It had long been conjectured that no map needs more than four colours, but it was not proved until 1976 when two American mathematicians gave a computer-based proof.

It is an interesting task to colour maps of English counties, European countries, American states using four colours.

References

K. Selkirk, *Pattern and Place* (Cambridge University Press)

R. Courant and H. Robbins, *What is Mathematics?* (Oxford University Press)

87 ▪ Music and mathematics

Many pupils would not think that music involves mathematical ideas. However, the physical basis of music can be expressed in mathematical laws, and patterns in musical form can be analysed mathematically. There are opportunities for pupils to explore these connections.

1 Strings

(a) Measure the distances of the frets of a guitar from the bridge.
Is there a relationship between the fret number and the distance? Plot a graph showing fret number against distance.

There should be an exponential relationship revealed by a constant multiplying factor. It arises for the following reason: The sound is caused by the vibration of string, column of air or membrane, the frequency of the vibration determining the pitch of the note. The frequency of a note is double the frequency of the note one octave lower in pitch. An octave in the chromatic scale is divided into twelve intervals (semitones) which are recognised by the ear as equal steps in pitch. The frequency of a note is therefore $2^{1/12}(\simeq 1.0595)$ times the frequency of the note one semitone lower. Putting it another way, since wavelength is inversely proportional to frequency, the wavelength of a note is approximately 1.0595 times the wavelength of the note one semitone higher.

(b) The frequency of a note emitted when a string is plucked depends on the length,

tension, and mass of the string. An experiment could be designed to investigate these relationships. Appropriate equipment is probably available in the physics department.

(c) Pythagoras is said to have been one of the first to study musical scales. He found that when the lengths of strings are ratios of simple whole numbers a harmonious sound is produced when the strings are plucked. An octave is the simplest example – a ratio of 2 : 1. The ratio 3 : 2 gives what is called a perfect fifth. The ratio 4 : 3 gives a perfect fourth.

Starting with middle C and going up in intervals of perfect fifths leads to the sequence G, D, A, E, B, F#, D♭, A♭, E♭, B♭, F, C. The first five of these notes – C, G, D, A, E – form the basis of the pentatonic scale which is used in some folk songs.

An interesting account of these ideas is given in *The Fascination of Groups* by F. Budden. Although the book is written for use at a higher level, much of the chapter on music is accessible to readers with a knowledge of music.

2 Notation for musical time intervals

Music is made up of sounds and silences. Find out about the notation used to code the time values of the sounds and silences.

What is the effect of a dot after a note?

What is meant by a time-signature?

What is a bar?

Examine some pieces of music to show how the duration of each bar is related to the time signature.

3 Musical form

Patterns often occur in the way a piece of music is written – an obvious example is a *round*. More complicated examples arise in canons and fugues. Sometimes a set of notes is repeated several times at different pitches giving a *sequence*.

The music of Bach and Handel is particularly rich in patterns. Further information with actual examples is given in *The Fascination of Groups*.

4 Bell-ringing

Bell-ringing is performed according to certain rules:

(a) Changes in the order of ringing can only be made by adjacent bells. For example, if six bells are rung in the order 1 2 3 4 5 6, the next sequence could be 1 3 2 4 5 6 but not 1 4 3 2 5 6.

(b) It is not usual for a bell to stay in the same position for more than two consecutive pulls.

It can be seen therefore that the analysis of bell-ringing involves the study of permutations.

With three bells all six possible permutations can easily be obtained using the rules (a) and (b). For four bells it is not as easy. *The Fascination of Groups* contains a chapter on campanology. The subject is discussed using groups but there is enough information to give ideas at a lower level.

5 Music and computers

Some microcomputers can be programmed to produce sounds. On the BBC Microcomputer a sound is defined by stating an amplitude, the pitch and the duration (and giving a 'channel' number). For example,

SOUND 1, −15, 53, 20

produces middle C lasting for 1 second.

The pitch and amplitude can be altered while the note is playing by using an 'envelope' command requiring 11 parameters which can be determined by graphing the pitch and amplitude.

Full details are given in the *BBC Microcomputer User Guide*.

References

F. Budden, *The Fascination of Groups* (out of print; Cambridge University Press)

F. W. Land, *The Language of Mathematics* (Murray)

Schools Council, Mathematics for the Majority, *Crossing Subject Boundaries* (Chatto and Windus)

J. Paynter and P. Aston, *Sound and Silence* (Cambridge University Press)

W. W. Sawyer, *Integrated Mathematics Scheme: Book C* (Bell and Hyman)

BBC Microcomputer User Guide (BBC)

88 ▪ Photography

Perusal of popular books on photography shows that there is a considerable amount of mathematics involved for anyone who takes the subject seriously. A project on photography can provide opportunities for enthusiasts and make useful links with the physics department.

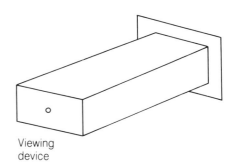

Viewing
device

1 The optics of cameras

(a) To understand how a camera works some appreciation of the physical principles of light and the mathematical transformation of enlargement are needed.

What is meant by the focal length of a lens?

What is the size of the angle from which a lens can take in light?

What is the effect of a telephoto lens?

What do the f numbers on a camera indicate?

What is the relationship between the numbers in the sequence 1.4, 2, 2.8, . . .?

What is meant by the depth of field? What factors need to be taken into account in order to allow for depth of field?

What are film *speeds*?

(b) Making models
   (i) Make a pinhole camera and explain the principle.
   (ii) Make a viewing device to see the amount of a subject which your camera will show: a small cardboard box whose length is the focal length of the lens with a frame at one end the size of a camera's picture format (for example, a colour slide mount) and a small hole at the other end.

   Alternatively, instead of using a box, the mount can be fitted onto a ruler so that it slides along. Then the amounts of the subject for lenses of different focal lengths can be compared.

(c) Flash photography
   What are flash factors?
   Some reflectors have elliptical sections, others are parabolic. What are their features?

(d) Close-up exposure
   Accurate focussing is essential. Many books include formulae, tables and nomograms to assist.

2 Enlarging

How does an enlarger work? How is the size of the enlargement determined?

3 The cost of photography

How much does a photograph cost? Compare the cost of sending a film away (by post or through a local shop) with doing your own developing.

References

M. Langford, *Better Photography* (Focal Press)
M. Freeman, *The Manual of Indoor Photography* (Macdonald)
D. Watkins, *SLR Photography* (David and Charles)

89 ▪ Crystals

The study of crystals and crystal structure occurs in some school chemistry courses. It involves interesting mathematical ideas which require an ability to see spatial patterns and can give rise to various projects.

1 Symmetries

Crystallography provides an opportunity for showing an application of polyhedra and symmetry. Many substances are made up of crystals which are in the form of polyhedra. For example, fluorite crystals are in the form of cubes, gold crystals are octahedra, pyrite crystals are dodecahedra. Crystals are classified according to their symmetries. Models of the crystals illustrated above can be made using card and cocktail sticks to show the symmetries.

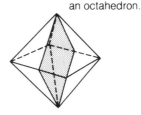

The two types of planes of symmetry of an octahedron.

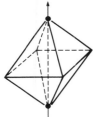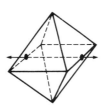

The three types of axes of symmetry of an octahedron.

2 Structure

A higher level project is to study crystal structure. Crystals can be thought of as made up of spheres packed together. The packing can take place in various ways.

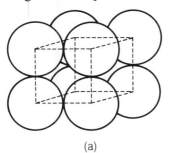

(a)

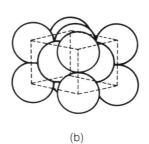

(b)

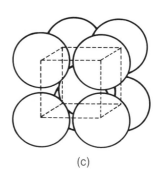

(c)

One problem of interest to chemists is to find how much space there is inside the 'cells' shown by the dotted lines in the above diagram. The cell in (a) is made up of 8 segments of spheres of radius r, each of which is an eighth of a sphere of radius r. The fraction of the cell occupied is

$$\frac{\frac{4}{3}\pi r^3}{(2r)^3} \simeq 0.52$$

Thus about half of the cell is empty space.

Using the enlarged versions of (b) and (c), and with the help of Pythagoras' theorem, it can be shown that the fraction of the cell occupied in (b) is 0.74 and in (c) is 0.68.

Is there a relationship between the number of spheres each sphere touches and the closeness of the packing?

Simple models of these crystal structures can be made with plasticine. For more permanent models, table-tennis balls can be used or polystyrene spheres (obtainable from the chemistry department).

(b) enlarged

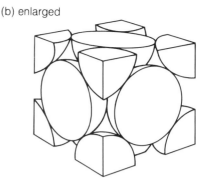

(c) enlarged

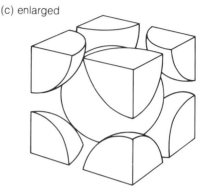

3 Lattice models

The crystal structure in (a) is often shown more clearly like this.

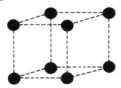

X-ray analysis has revealed that there are 14 different structures. A set of models can be made to illustrate them.

References

A. F. Wells, *The Third Dimension in Chemistry* (Oxford University Press)

F. C. Philips, *An Introduction to Crystallography* (Oliver and Boyd)

A. Windell, *A First Course in Crystallography* (Bell)

M. Gardner, *The Ambidextrous Universe* (Penguin)

H. Steinhaus, *Mathematical Snapshots* (Oxford University Press)

Open University, TS 251, *An Introduction to Materials, Unit 2: The Architecture of Solids*, pp. 30–4

J. Ling, *Mathematics across the Curriculum* (Blackie)

90 ▪ Random numbers

The technique of simulation can be used to investigate various problems in which random events occur – for example, traffic flow, queues, etc. For this purpose random numbers are needed. A project could be based on methods for generating random numbers.

1 Some simple methods

(a) Throw a die.
(b) Pick cards from a pack of playing cards.
(c) Toss coins (for example, tossing three different coins, and representing a head by 1, and a tail by 0, to give binary numbers from 000 to 111, i.e. 0 to 7 in base ten).
(d) Make a spinner in the form of a regular polygon.
(e) Dice in the form of polyhedra other than cubes are available from some educational suppliers. Alternatively, home-made polyhedra can be used.
  Invent some more methods.
  Suppose random numbers from 1 to 20 are required. Devise efficient methods for obtaining such numbers using dice, etc.

2 Checking for randomness

- Find the relative frequency of each digit.
- Find the relative frequency of pairs of digits.
- Find the 'gaps' between successive occurrences of 1, say.
- Compare your results with theory.
(a) Tables of random numbers are available in books of mathematical tables and in books on statistics. Check them for randomness.

(b) Many scientific calculators have random number generators which produce a random decimal between 0.000 and 0.999. The decimal point can be ignored and each digit can be used as a random number from 0 to 9. They can be tested for randomness.
(c) Computers have random number generators. Write a short program to test for randomness.
(d) Calculators and computers must obtain their random numbers by some deterministic process – they cannot therefore be random in the true sense of the word. Find out how they are generated.

3 Print your own tables

Use a computer to print out a table of 1000 random digits with 50 digits per line arranged in sets of 5.

4 A computer simulation

Use a computer to simulate throwing a die and to record the results in a frequency table and to draw a bar chart.
  The program could be extended for throwing two (or three) dice and adding the top numbers. Comparison could be made with theory.

References

D. Cooke, A. H. Craven and G. M. Clarke, *Basic Statistical Computing* (Arnold)

J. Lighthill (ed.), *Newer Uses of Mathematics* (Penguin)

SMP 11–16, *Book YE2* (Cambridge University Press)

91 ▪ Simulating movement

Random numbers can be used to determine directions of movement. Two examples of this application are given here.

1 Radiation shielding

This is a simple model of an atomic pile. In order to provide protection the atomic pile at O is surrounded by concrete. Neutrons generated at O move up, down, left or right with equal probabilities once every second.

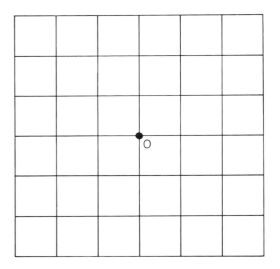

If a neutron reaches the boundary in 5 seconds or less, it escapes, but, if it has not reached the boundary in that time, its energy has been dissipated and it is absorbed. What fraction of neutrons escape?

A simulation can be carried out by tossing a coin twice:

HH	move right
TT	move left
HT	move up
TH	move down

Alternatively, random numbers or a calculator could be used:

even, even   move right
odd, odd   move left
etc.

Some possible variations:

(a) Experiment with other thicknesses of concrete. How thick should the concrete be so that it is unlikely that more than 5% of neutrons escape?

(b) How long does it take on average for neutrons to escape?

(c) Suppose that instead of having a life of 5 seconds a neutron could be absorbed at any stage with a probability of $\frac{1}{8}$.

(d) Invent a three-dimensional version.

Computer programs could be written to simulate these problems. Graphics effects could be used.

2 The spread of Dutch elm disease

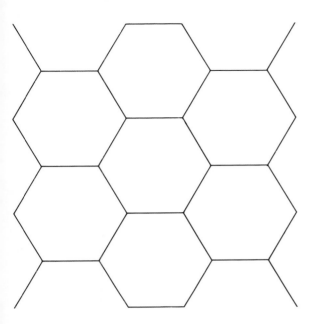

A simple model can be made using a hexagonal grid. In each time interval the disease spreads from one hexagon to a neighbouring hexagon determined by a random number 1, 2, 3, 4, 5, 6, which can conveniently be obtained by throwing a die.

The spread of the disease after various numbers of time intervals can be investigated.

Alternatively, a square grid can be used as for the radiation shielding simulation.

Again, computer programs could be written. The hexagonal grid requires the use of non-rectangular coordinates.

Various other contexts for spread can be devised.

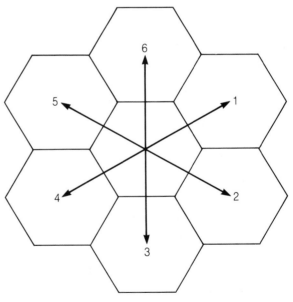

References

K. Selkirk, *Pattern and Place*, chapter 22 (Cambridge University Press)

F. R. Watson, *A Simple Introduction to Simulation* (Keele Mathematics Education Publications)

92 · Simulating the lifetime of an electrical device

An electrical device consists of three bulbs connected in series. When one bulb fails the device is no longer of use. The problem is to estimate the average life of the device.

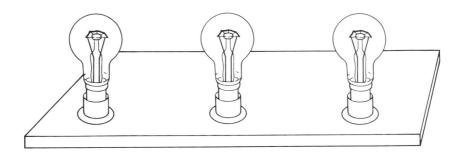

1 A simple simulation

An assumption will need to be made about the lifetimes of each bulb. As a first model, assume that the bulbs have lifetimes which are equally likely to be 1, 2, 3, . . ., 10 hours. A simulation can then be carried out using a table of random numbers or a calculator with a random number facility (0 representing 10 hours). The random digits can be taken in sets of three, each digit giving the lifetime of a bulb. Record the least digit of the three to represent the lifetime of the whole device. Carry out the simulation 100 times, say, and find the mean lifetime.

2 Extensions of the simulation

(a) Other distributions for the lifetime of each bulb can be devised. For example, 5% of length 1, 8% of length 2, etc.
(b) Other numbers of components can be used.

3 Using a computer

A computer program can be written to simulate the device. For the simple version, three random numbers will need to be generated and the smallest of them determined.

With the equally-likely assumption the theoretical distribution of lifetimes can be calculated. The appropriate geometrical picture is a cubical lattice of 1000 points. The points which give a lifetime of 1 can be obtained as the difference between two cubes: there are $10^3 - 9^3 = 271$ such points. The probability that the lifetime of the device is 1 is therefore $\frac{271}{1000}$. Similarly the probabilities of the other lifetimes can be calculated from differences between two cubes.

With other assumptions about individual lifetimes it is more difficult to calculate probabilities theoretically, and it is then that the method of simulation is helpful.

References

P. G. Moore, *Reason by Numbers* (Penguin)

93 ▪ Queues

Simulations are often used to investigate queueing problems which do not admit a simple theoretical analysis.

1 Doctor's surgery

Appointments to see a doctor are made at ten-minute intervals from 9:00 a.m. to 10:50 a.m. Consultations take from 5 to 14 minutes, each time 5, 6, . . ., 14 minutes (to the nearest minute) being equally likely.

Some simplifying assumptions will need to be made. For example:
- Patients arrive on time;
- If the doctor is free, he sees a patient immediately on arrival;
- The doctor always finishes off any consultation started before 11:00 a.m.;
- Patients who have not been seen by 11:00 a.m. are sent away.

Random numbers 0, 1, . . ., 9 can be used to represent the consultation times 5, 6, . . ., 14 minutes.

A clear method for recording the simulation will need to be devised.

Some possible questions to investigate are:
- What is the average waiting time for a patient?
- For how much time is the doctor idle?
- How many patients do not get seen?

Various modifications can be tried out:
- To avoid idle time at the beginning book in two patients at 9:00 a.m.
- Allow for patients not turning up. For example, suppose the probability is 0.1 that a patient does not attend.
- Suppose 70% of patients arrive on time, 20% arrive 5 minutes early, and 10% arrive 5 minutes late.
- Try other distributions of consulting times.

Pupils with programming experience could write a computer program to carry out the simulation. Commercial software for simulations of this type is also available.

2 Post office or bank

This simulation will not involve appointments. Assumptions will need to be made about the probability of an arrival in fixed time intervals and about the distribution of service times.

The model could be extended to involve more than one service point.

A simulation of a local post office or bank could be carried out by first doing a survey to find the average rate of arrival and the average service times.

Is it best to allow customers to go to any service point or to have a single queue from which people proceed to a vacant service point?

3 Other queues

Find some other queueing situations and try to simulate them. For example, queues at shops, railway stations, bus stops, petrol stations, traffic queues, etc.

References

SMP 11–16, *Book YE2* (Cambridge University Press)

K. Ruthven, *The Maths Factory* (Cambridge University Press)

94 · Letter counts

The frequency with which the different letters of the alphabet occur in any piece of written English is quite significant and has been taken account of in a variety of situations. The first activity is about finding the relative frequency of the letters and is the basis of all the others. Because of the amount of work involved when all the letters of the alphabet are considered it is best used as a group activity.

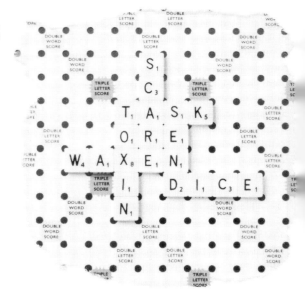

1 Relative frequencies

Make letter counts of different letters of the alphabet:
- How many 'e's occur in 1000 letters?
- Compare the number of occurrences of the vowels.
- Which letters occur most frequently, which the least?
- Does the relative frequency differ with (a) different authors, (b) different languages?

Use bar charts, pie charts or pictograms to represent your findings.

2 Games using letters

There are many popular games which depend on the players making up words using letters which are on: individual cards such as in Lexicon or Kan-U-Go; tiles as in Scrabble; faces of dice as in Shake Words or Boggle. For these games to be playable the proportion of vowels to consonants and the frequency of occurrence of the letters in the playing pieces should match their use in the English language. How is this achieved?

In Lexicon and Scrabble different values are attached to different letters. What is the logic behind the values given?

Design a new letter/word game.

3 Morse code

In the Morse code, each letter is represented by a sequence of 'dots' and 'dashes'. Is there any relationship between the frequency with which the letter is used and the number of 'dots' and 'dashes' used in its code?

Similar questions can be asked about how the different letters are represented (a) in Braille, (b) in binary for a teleprinter, (c) in a computer.

4 The typewriter keyboard

How is the design of a typewriter keyboard related to the frequency with which the letters are used? Could you suggest/design a better keyboard?

References

Commercial word games such as Scrabble, Shake Words, Boggle, Kan-U-Go, Lexicon
Encyclopedias
A. B. Bolt and M. E. Wardle, *Communicating with a Computer* (Cambridge University Press)
The Spode Group, *Solving Real Problems with CSE Mathematics* (Cranfield Press)

95 - Comparing newspapers

How does a 'popular' paper (such as the *Sun* or the *Daily Mirror*) differ from a 'quality' paper (such as *The Times* or the *Guardian*)?

1 What is regarded as *news*? How much space is given to
- international news
- politics
- human interest stories
- sport

etc.?

2 What fraction (or percentage) consists of
- photographs
- advertisements?

3 Compare the balance of photographs of men and women.

4 Do they give value for money? (How do you measure value? A survey of what people are looking for in a newspaper might be needed.)

5 Are there many misprints?

6 Compare the style of writing
- the distribution of sentence lengths
- the distribution of word lengths
- the fraction of sentences which are short
- the fraction of sentences which are long

etc.

If you were given a passage from a newspaper, could you tell which paper it was from? (The passage would need to be re-typed so that the newspaper could not be identified from the print face.)

7 Consider similar questions about (a) free papers, (b) colour supplements, (c) women's magazines. In particular find the amount of space given to advertisements.

96 ▪ Sorting by computer

One of the main uses of a computer is in data processing – for example, maintaining records about all the employees in a factory. At some stage an alphabetical list of employees might be required. It is then necessary for the computer to go through the list of employees and sort the names into alphabetical order. Again, at school alphabetical lists of different types are often required. The process of sorting can be very time-consuming.

A project for students familiar with programming is to devise and compare various sorting methods.

1 Devising a method by experiment

To appreciate the problem write names on ten pieces of paper, shuffle them and place them name-down on a table from left to right. By comparing two items at a time arrange the names in alphabetical order. Devise various methods.

Alternatively, sort a set of ten books into alphabetical order by author. Devise various methods and write sets of instructions (flow diagrams) for them.

A computer program for this is as follows. It assumes that the names have been stored as A\$(1), A\$(2), . . ., A\$(N).

```
100 FOR J = 1 TO N−1
110 FOR K = J+1 TO N
120 IF A$(J) > A$(K) THEN B$ = A$(J) :
    A$(J) = A$(K) : A$(K) = B$
130 NEXT K
140 NEXT J
```

Various standard methods are described in the references.

2 A computer sort

A possible method is to compare the first item on the left with the second, interchange if necessary, then compare the item in first place with the third one, interchange if necessary and so on. This gets the first item correct.

The procedure is then repeated with the second item, comparing it with those on its right. The second item is then correct.

Next the third item is compared with those on its right and so on.

References

B. H. Blakeley, *Data Processing* (Cambridge University Press)

D. Cooke, A. H. Craven and G. M. Clarke, *Basic Statistical Computing* (Arnold)

97 · Weighted networks

A topological network is often drawn showing the connections between various geographical points. Numbers can then be associated with each arc of the network corresponding, for example, to the distances between the nodes or the time taken to travel between the nodes or the number of telephone lines connecting the nodes. With these interpretations a variety of problems pose themselves whose solutions are of practical and commercial importance. A project which addresses itself to one or more of these problems has many possibilities.

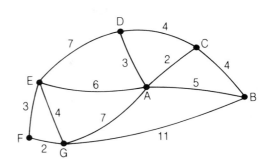

1 Shortest connection

Treating the numbers as distances and the nodes as villages find the minimum length of gas main the gas company would need to lay to interconnect all the villages. The problem is one of deciding which of the arcs to leave out of the network without isolating any village and at the same time minimising the total length of the arcs used.

In this example the best solution is the one shown here. Did you find it? More important, in solving it, could you see a strategy which will enable you to solve all similar problems? See activity 101 in *EMMA* for an explanation.

2 Road inspection

Taking the arcs as representing the streets to be walked by a police officer on her beat and the numbers on the arcs as the time in minutes it takes to walk each street, what route should be followed to minimise the total time to walk all the streets if she starts and finishes at A?

If the network was traversible then the solution would be easy, but it is not. The solution however depends on understanding the conditions for a network to be traversible and then effectively turning the network into a

traversible network by doubling up some of
the arcs. See activities 100 and 45 in *EMMA*
and activity 48 in *MA*.

The miminum time in this example is 65
minutes and can be achieved by

$$A \rightarrow G \rightarrow B \rightarrow C \rightarrow B \rightarrow A \rightarrow C \rightarrow D \rightarrow A \rightarrow D \rightarrow E \rightarrow F \rightarrow G \rightarrow E \rightarrow A.$$
$$\quad 7 \quad 11 \quad 4 \quad 4 \quad 5 \quad 2 \quad 4 \quad 3 \quad 3 \quad 7 \quad 3 \quad 2 \quad 4 \quad 6$$

3 Travelling salesman's problem

An international diplomat based at B wishes
to visit all the capital cities represented by the
nodes of the network. The numbers on the
arcs represent the hours in flying time along
each route. How would you advise the
diplomat to travel to minimise the flying time?
It can be achieved in 32 hours in four ways.
Can you suggest any general strategies for
solving this kind of problem? See activity 65 in
EMMA.

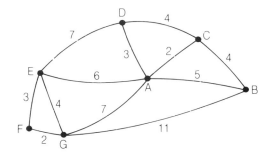

4 Shortest route and longest route

The shortest route between any two nodes of
the network is a fairly obvious problem with a
simple network like that given but in a more
complex network, especially when some arcs
are arrowed to make them 'one-way' as in city
streets, life becomes more interesting.

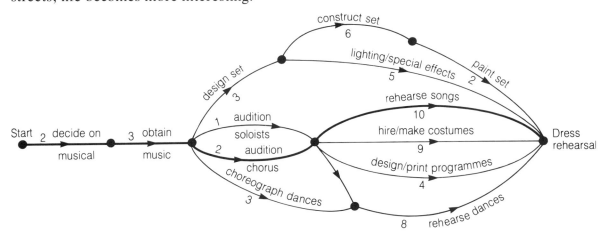

If the nodes represent events in time like the opening night of the school musical and the numbers on the arrows represent the time (in weeks) say between ordering the costumes and their arrival, then the complex process of mounting a musical can be represented by a directed network and the longest path through it, known as the *critical path*, is of particular significance and gives the shortest time in which the musical can be mounted.

5 Maximum flow

Assuming the nodes of the original network correspond to telephone exchanges and the numbers on the arcs correspond to the number of lines joining the exchanges to each other, investigate the maximum number of telephone subscribers to G who could talk to subscribers at C at the same time. See activity 102 in *EMMA*.

References

B. Bolt, *Even More Mathematical Activities (EMMA)*, and *Mathematical Activities (MA)* (Cambridge University Press)

The Spode Group, *Decision Maths Pack* (Edward Arnold)

The Spode Group, *A-level Decision Mathematics* (Ellis Horwood)

A. Battersby, *Mathematics in Management* (Penguin)

A. Fletcher and G. Clarke, *Management and Mathematics* (Business Publications)

98 ▪ Codes

Many pupils will at some stage have sent secret messages using codes. The idea is by no means trivial – language itself is a code – and there are numerous aspects which can form the basis of a project.

1 Secret messages

(a) A simple method of coding is to replace each letter by the letter three places on, say, in the alphabet. This is often called a Caesar code, named after Julius Caesar who is said to have sent messages in this way. Decode the message shown here.

```
WKLV    LVDQ
HDVB    FRGH
WRFV    DFN
```

A device for a code of this type can be made from two strips of paper:

```
ABCDEFGHIJKLMNOPQRSTUVWXYZ
ABCDEFGHIJKLMNOPQRSTUVWXYZABCDEFGHIJ
```

Alternatively, a circular version can be made with a disc of card rotating on a larger disc.

(b) A code which is more difficult to crack can be made by replacing each letter with another letter but not chosen according to a rule as in (a). In order to crack the code the frequency of each letter in the message needs to be found and then the information from Project 94 can be used to make conjectures about the most common letters. Some trial and error is needed.

It is interesting to check the frequencies of letters in other languages, such as French.

Use is made of the frequencies of letters in the Sherlock Holmes story *The Dancing Man*.

(c) Some other interesting methods for coding messages are given in the references.

(d) Codes are used by spies and in warfare. One of the classic examples is the message sent by a Japanese spy in 1941

```
BEVAP QOZVE HBBZX VPFZP AEBWZ DENVT JVWBA

BZVWZ BQNZW ZVOBG TAABJ BYVWZ DENJB ZVOVE

WFBGE AWBHD NTVWJ ZBGJV WBJVV OZPWH DNTVW

OPJAB DENDW OPJJW DTTJE BODEN PJZVJ WGYHV

ABIVF WZVOZ DWVKB FVJWW FPMSP EAZVV UHVMW

VAWBK DEAHD NTVWO PFYDE NZDJW BVJDE KFBEW

BKZDJ KDFVX GWNBZ DJJGF HFDJV ZVJPO WZPWW

ZVABB FOPJB HVEPE AWZVY BFVZV TBBSV ADEJD

AVWZV YBFVH DNTVW OPJEW WZVFV
```

just before the bombing of Pearl Harbour in the United States.

In World War II the Germans designed a coding machine called ENIGMA which worked by a combination of mechanical and electrical devices. The cracking of this machine by British intelligence enabled many secret messages to be decoded. Further information is in *Top Secret Ultra* by Peter Calvocoressi.

2 Some useful codes

(a) The Morse code was invented in order that messages could be sent by electrical means.

(b) The Braille alphabet is a code which enables blind people to read words using their fingers.

(c) Shorthand is a code which can be written rapidly by secretaries.

(d) Books are coded by ISBN numbers (International Standard Book Number). For example, the ISBN for this book is 0 521 34759 9. The first digit 0 identifies the language group, the next three digits 521 indicate the publisher, Cambridge University Press, and the next five are allocated by the publisher for this particular book. The last digit is a check digit, chosen so that

$$0 \times 10$$
$$+ 5 \times 9$$
$$+ 2 \times 8$$
$$+ 1 \times 7$$
$$+ 3 \times 6$$
$$+ 4 \times 5$$
$$+ 7 \times 4$$
$$+ 5 \times 3$$
$$+ 9 \times 2$$
$$+ 9 \times 1 \, (= 176)$$

is 0 mod 11.

Bookshops order books using the ISBN numbers. If an error is made in transmitting the number it will (usually) be shown up by a computer check – the result of the above calculation would not come to 0 mod 11.

(e) Books such as this one and many other items bought in shops have a bar code and an article number. At the checkout this bar code is scanned by a laser beam and a message is sent to a computer which holds the prices of all the items. Appropriate details then appear on the display unit at the checkout and are printed on the till receipt.

The numbers on the article code are made up like this:

97	80521	34759	4
Country code	Manufacturer reference	Product number	Check digit

The check digit is determined as follows
find the sum X of the 6 digits in odd positions (counting from the left)
find the sum Y of the 6 digits in even positions
Then the check digit is such that
$X - Y + $ check digit $= 0$ mod 10

By collecting the codes from packets, etc. the codes for products of various countries and manufacturers can be deduced.

Cracking the code for the bars provides an interesting challenge. Information is available from Article Numbering Association (UK) Ltd.

References

A. Sinkov, *Elementary Cryptanalysis* (The Mathematical Association of America)
J. Pearcy and K. Lewis, *Experiments in Mathematics: Stage 2* (Longman)
Leapfrogs, *Codes* (Tarquin)
W. W. Rouse Ball, *Mathematical Recreations and Essays* (Macmillan)
P. Calvocoressi, *Top Secret Ultra* (Cassell)
The Spode Group, *Solving Problems with CSE Mathematics* (Cranfield Press)

99 ▪ Computer codes

Since computers work on a two-state system (a current is either flowing or not flowing, a switch is either on or off) it is convenient to represent numbers and letters in binary code.

1 Paper tape

Find out how characters were represented on paper tape. Explain why on eight-track tape there is always an even number of holes on each line.

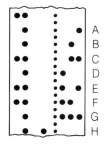

2 The ASCII code

Microcomputers use the ASCII character code (American Standard Code for Information Interchange) in which symbols are represented by a seven-bit 'word' called a byte. For example, A is 1000001. These words can be written more compactly as hexadecimal numbers (i.e. base sixteen): 1000001 becomes 41. Symbols then have to be invented for ten, eleven, twelve, thirteen, fourteen and fifteen: the letters A, B, C, D, E, F are used. Hexadecimal numbers can be seen on a microcomputer screen when a tape is being loaded.

The symbol corresponding to a hexadecimal number can be found using, for example, PRINT CHR$(&41).

Find out more about the ASCII code, the hexadecimal system and related computer instructions.

3 Graphics codes

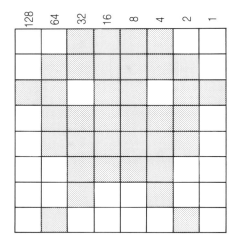

Graphics characters on a BBC micro are coded using a binary principle. For example, the space invader shown here is coded by thinking of the top line as 00111100 in binary, which is 60 in base ten. The second line is 01111110 in binary, which is 126 in base ten. And so on.

This program prints the space invader at position (500, 600):
```
10 MODE 5
20 VDU 23,240,60,126,219,126,60,36,66
30 VDU 5
40 MOVE 500,600
50 PRINT CHR$(240)
```
Invent some graphics characters and find out how to animate them.

References

P. Craddock and A. R. Haskins, *An Introduction to Computer Studies* (Wheaton)
BBC Microcomputer User Guide (BBC)

100 ▪ Maximising capacity

A commonly occurring problem is to fit as many items as possible into a given amount of space. Three contexts in which it arises are given below.

1 The library

A room measuring 8 metres by 10 metres is available for use as a library at your school. Design shelving to accommodate as many books as possible.

Assumptions will need to be made about the positions of windows and doors. Space will be needed for the issue and return of books. Shelves must be accessible without the use of steps.

Alternatively, improve the arrangements in the school library or a local library in order to maximise the number of books.

2 Fast-food restaurants

Fast-food restaurants usually try to fit in as many tables as possible. Design a suitable arrangement for a restaurant measuring 5 metres by 8 metres. Allow space for doors and give consideration to space for movement.

3 Desks in a hall

A problem which might occur at school is to get as many desks as possible into a hall for an examination.

Find out the regulations about the minimum distance between desks and then maximise the number of desks which can be put in the halls or rooms used for examinations in your school.

101 • The school

There are many aspects about attendance at school and behavioural patterns which are worthy of study. Some projects could be presented as displays for parents' evenings or as reports for the school governors.

1 Where do pupils attending the school live? Devise a system for showing where they live on a map. What is the average distance from school? Find out about the catchment areas of other local schools. Is there a need for more schools or for fewer?

2 How do pupils come to school? Walk, cycle, bus, train, car? How long does it take them? What time do they leave home? Is there a connection between the time and the distance they have to travel?

3 Find out which primary schools pupils attended. Study the distribution of primary schools in your locality. Is it related to the density of population?

4 Find out about projected numbers for the future. Make recommendations about the consequences of an increase or a decrease (for example, changes in the number of rooms and teachers required).

5 If in your area there is a proposal to close a small village school, quantify the effect of sending children to neighbouring schools.

6 Obtain information about absences from school. What is the average absence rate? Does the number of absences depend on the day of the week?

7 How long do pupils spend on homework? How long do they spend watching television? Is there a relationship between these times?

8 What do pupils eat for school dinners? Do they choose nutritious food? How are the meals planned?

References

Andrews, W. S., *Magic Squares and Cubes* (Dover)

Arnold, P. (ed.), *The Complete Book of Indoor Games* (Hamlyn)

Arnold, P., *The Encyclopedia of Gambling* (Collins)

Ballinger, L. B., *Perspective, Space and Design* (Van Nostrand Reinhold)

BBC Microcomputer User Guide (BBC)

Battersby, A., *Mathematics in Management* (Penguin)

Beckett, D., *Brunel's Britain* (David and Charles)

Bender, A. E., *Calories and Nutrition* (Mitchell Beazley)

Blake, J., *How to Solve Your Interior Design Problems* (Hamlyn)

Blakeley, B. H., *Data Processing* (Cambridge University Press)

Blue Peter, *Fourteenth Annual* (BBC)

Bolt, B., *Even More Mathematical Activities* (Cambridge University Press)

Bolt, B., *Mathematical Activities* (Cambridge University Press)

Bolt, B., *More Mathematical Activities* (Cambridge University Press)

Bolt, A. B., and Wardle, M. E., *Communicating with a Computer* (Cambridge University Press)

Bond, J. (ed.), *The Good Food Growing Guide* (David and Charles)

Boyer, C., *A History of Mathematics* (Wiley)

Brooke, M., *Tricks, Games and Puzzles with Matches* (Dover)

The Buckminster Fuller Reader (Penguin)

Buckminster Fuller, R., *Synergetics* (Macmillan)

Budden, F., *The Fascination of Groups* (Cambridge University Press; out of print)

Burton, A., *Canals in Colour* (Blandford)

Caket, C., *An Introduction to Perspective* (Macmillan Educational)

Caket, C., *Getting Things into Perspective* (Macmillan Educational)

Campbell, W. R., and Tucker, N. M., *An Introduction to Tests and Measurement in Physical Education* (Bell)

Calvocoressi, P., *Top Secret Ultra* (Cassell)

Clare, T., *Archaeological Sites of Devon and Cornwall* (Moorland Publishing)

Cooke, D., Craven, A. H., and Clarke, G. M., *Basic Statistical Computing* (Arnold)

Couling, D., *The AAA Esso Five Star Award Scheme Scoring Tables* (D. Couling, 102 High Street, Castle Donnington, Derby)

Courant, R., and Robbins, H., *What is Mathematics?* (Oxford University Press)

Craddock, P., and Haskins, A. R., *An Introduction to Computer Studies* (Wheaton)

Cruden's Complete Concordance to the Old and New Testaments (Lutterworth)

Cundy, H. M., and Rollett, A. P., *Mathematical Models* (Tarquin)

Daish, C. B., *The Physics of Ball Games* (English Universities Press)

D'Arcy Thompson, *On Growth and Form* (Cambridge University Press)

Derraugh, P. and W., *Wedding Etiquette* (Foulsham)

Diagram Group, *The Book of Comparisons* (Penguin)

Dickinson, N., *English Schools Athletic Association Handbook* (N. Dickinson, 26 Coniscliffe Road, Stanley, Co Durham, DH9 7RF)

Donald, P., *The Pony Trap* (Weidenfeld and Nicholson)

Dubery, F., and Willats, J., *Perspective and Other Drawing Systems* (Herbert Press)

Dudeney, H. E., *Amusements in Mathematics* (Dover)

Elfers, J., *Tangram: The Ancient Chinese Shapes Game* (Penguin)

Energy Efficiency Office, *Make the Most of Your Heating* and *Cutting Home Energy Costs* (Energy Efficiency Office, Room 1312, Thames House South, Millbank, London SW1P 4QJ)

Ernst, B., *Adventures with Impossible Figures* (Tarquin)

Erricker, B. C., *Elementary Statistics* (Hodder)

Escher, M. C., *The Graphic Work of M. C. Escher* (Pan)

Exchange and Mart Guide to Buying Your Secondhand Car

Exploring Mathematics on Your Own: Curves (John Murray)

Exploring Mathematics on Your Own: The World of Measurement (John Murray)

Eykyn, J. W. W., *All You Need to Know About Loft Conversions* (Collins)

Fishburn, A., *The Batsford Book of Lampshades* (Batsford)

Fletcher, A., and Clarke, G. *Management and Mathematics* (Business Publications)

Football League Tables (Collins)

Freeman, M., *The Manual of Indoor Photography* (Macdonald)

Gardner, M., *Further Mathematical Diversions* (Penguin)

Gardner, M., *Mathematical Carnival* (Penguin)

Gardner, M., *Mathematical Circus* (Penguin)

Gardner, M., *Mathematical Puzzles and Diversions* (Penguin)

Gardner, M., *Mathematics, Magic and Mystery* (Dover)

Gardner, M., *More Mathematical Puzzles and Diversions* (Penguin)

Gardner, M., *New Mathematical Diversions* (Allen and Unwin)

Gardner, M., *The Ambidextrous Universe* (Penguin)

Genders, R., *The Allotment Garden* (John Gifford)

Gibbons, R. F., and Blofield, B. A., *Life Size* (Macmillan; out of print)

Gilliland, J., *Readability* (University of London Press)

Goldwater, D., *Bridges and How They are Built* (World's Work Ltd)

Golomb, S. W., *Polyominoes* (Allen and Unwin)

Gombrich, E., *The Story of Art* (Phaidon)

Gordon, J. E., *Structures* (Penguin)

Guinness Book of Records (Guinness Superlatives)

Grafton, C., *Geometric Patchwork Patterns* (Dover)

Haldane, J. B. S., *On Being the Right Size* (Oxford University Press)

Harbin, R., *Origami* (Hodder)

Harrison, C., *Readability in the Classroom* (Cambridge University Press)

Haskins, M. J., *Evaluation in Physical Education* (W. C. Brown)

Hogben, L., *Man Must Measure* (Rathbone)

Hogben, L., *Mathematics for the Million* (Pan)

How Things Work: The Universal Encyclopedia of Machines, vols. 1 and 2 (Paladin)

Holding, J., *Mathematical Roses* (Cambridge Microsoftware: Cambridge University Press)

Homerton College, *Tessellations* (Cambridge Microsoftware: Cambridge University Press)

Huff, D., *How to Take a Chance* (Penguin)

IAAF, *Scoring Tables for Men's and Women's Combined Event Competitions* (International Amateur Athletics Federation)

Johnson, B. L., and Nelson, J. K., *Practical Measurements for Evaluation in Physical Education* (Burgess)

Johnson, W. H., *Beginner's Guide to Central Heating* (Newnes)

Kline, M., *Mathematics in Western Culture* (Oxford University Press)

Kraitchik, M., *Mathematical Recreations* (Allen and Unwin)

Land, F. W., *The Language of Mathematics* (Allen and Unwin)

Langford, M., *Better Photography* (Focal Press)

Leapfrogs, *Codes* (Tarquin)

Leapfrogs, *Curves* (Tarquin)

Lent, D., *Analysis and Design of Mechanisms* (Prentice Hall)

Lewis, D., *Teach Yourself: Buying, Selling and Moving Home* (Hodder and Stoughton)

Life Science Library: *Energy* (Time Life)

Life Science Library: *Machines* (Time Life)

Life Science Library: *Sound and Hearing* (Time Life)

Life Science Library: *Time* (Time Life)

Life Science Library: *Water* (Time Life)

Lindgren, H., *Recreational Problems in Geometric Dissections and How to Solve Them* (Dover)

Lighthill, J. (ed.), *Newer Uses of Mathematics* (Penguin)

Ling, J., *Mathematics Across the Curriculum* (Blackie)

Lockwood, E. H., *A Book of Curves* (Cambridge University Press)

Maré, E. de, *Bridges of Britain* (Batsford)

Mathematical Association, *132 Short Programs for the Mathematics Classroom* (Mathematical Association/Stanley Thornes)

Matthews, P. (ed.), *Athletics: The International Track and Field Annual* (Simon Schuster)

Matthews, P., *Guinness Track and Field Athletics – The Records* (Guinness Superlatives)

McKim, R., *101 Patchwork Patterns* (Dover)

Ministry of Transport, *Driving* (HMSO)

Ministry of Transport, *The Highway Code* (HMSO)

Molian, S., *Mechanism Design* (Cambridge University Press)

Moore, P. G., *Reason by Numbers* (Penguin)

Mottershead, L., *Sources of Mathematical Discovery* (Blackwell)

News of the World Football Yearbook (News of the World)

Netherhall Software, *Balance Your Diet* (Cambridge University Press)

Nieswand, N., *The Complete Interior Designer* (Macdonald Orbis)

Northrop, E. R., *Riddles in Mathematics* (Penguin)

O'Beirne, T. H., *Puzzles and Paradoxes* (Oxford University Press)

Open University, PME 233 *Mathematics Across the Curriculum, Unit 3: Measuring* (Open University)

Open University, TS 251 *An Introduction to Materials, Unit 2: The Architecture of Solids* (Open University)

Parker's Car Price Guide

Paynter, J., and Aston, P., *Sound and Silence* (Cambridge University Press)

Peak District National Park (HMSO)

Pearcy, J., and Lewis, K., *Experiments in Mathematics, Stage 2* (Longman)

Philips, F. C., *An Introduction to Crystallography* (Oliver and Boyd)

Playfair Football Annual (Queen Anne Press)

Powell, F., *A Consumer's Guide to Holidays Abroad* (Telegraph Publications)

Reader's Digest, *Illustrated Book of Dogs*

Reed, R. C., *Tangram: 330 Puzzles* (Tarquin)

Rothman's Football Yearbook (Queen Anne Press)

Rouse Ball, W. W., *Mathematical Recreations and Essays* (Macmillan)

Ruthven, K., *The Maths Factory* (Cambridge University Press)

Saunders, K., *Hexagrams* (Tarquin)

Sawyer, W. W., *Integrated Mathematics Scheme Book C* (Bell and Hyman)

School Mathematics Project – see SMP

Schools Council, Mathematics for the Majority Project, *Crossing Subject Boundaries* (Chatto and Windus)

Schools Council, Mathematics for the Majority Project, *Machines, Mechanisms and Mathematics* by B. Bolt and J. Hiscocks (Chatto and Windus)

Schools Council, Mathematics for the Majority Project, *Mathematics from Outdoors* (Chatto and Windus)

Schools Council, Modular Courses in Technology: *Mechanisms* (Oliver and Boyd)

Schools Council, Statistics in Your World: *On the Ball*, *Practice Makes Perfect* and *Retail Price Index* (Foulsham Educational)

Selkirk, K., *Pattern and Place* (Cambridge University Press)

Sherlock, A. J., *An Introduction to Probability and Statistics* (Arnold)

Shooter, K., and Saxton, J., *Making Things Work: An Introduction to Design Technology* (Cambridge University Press)

Shuard, H., and Rothery, A., *Children Reading Mathematics* (John Murray)

Sigma Project, *Billiards* (Hodder and Stoughton)

Sinkov, A., *Elementary Cryptanalysis* (The Mathematical Association of America)

Smith, T., *The Story of Measurement* (Blackwell)

SMP, *Book 1* (Cambridge University Press)

SMP, *Book E (Teacher's Guide)*, *Book G* (Cambridge University Press)

SMP, *New Book 4 Part 2*, *New Book 5* (Cambridge University Press)

SMP 11–16, *Books Y2, Y5, YE2, B2, B5* (Cambridge University Press)

SMP 11–16 G series, *Impossible Objects* (Cambridge University Press)

Spode Group, *A-Level Decision Mathematics* (Ellis Horwood)

Spode Group, *Decision Maths Pack* (Edward Arnold)

Spode Group, *GCSE Coursework Assignments* (Hodder and Stoughton)

Spode Group, *Solving Real Problems with CSE Mathematics* (Cranfield Press)

Spode Group, *Solving Real Problems with Mathematics*, vols. 1 and 2 (Cranfield Press)

Steinhaus, H., *Mathematical Snapshots* (Oxford University Press)

Stevens, P. S., *Patterns in Nature* (Penguin)

Strandh, S., *Machines, An Illustrated History* (Nordbok)

The Trachtenburg Speed System (Pan)

Index

The numbers refer to the **projects**, not to the pages.